Grace in Action

GRACE
IN ACTION

RICHARD ROHR, OFM
· *AND OTHERS* ·

Edited by Terry Carney and Christina Spahn

CROSSROAD · NEW YORK

1994
The Crossroad Publishing Company
370 Lexington Avenue, New York, NY 10017

Printed in the United States of America

Library of Congress Cataloging-in-Publication Data

Grace in action / by Richard Rohr and others.
    p. cm.
   "A compilation of the best writings from Radical Grace"—CIP data
sheet.
   ISBN 0-8245-1379-7
   1. Grace (Theology)   I. Rohr, Richard. II. Radical Grace.
BT761.2.G69   1994
230'.2—dc20   94–18074
                                                     CIP

With heartfelt gratitude
to
Fr. Richard Rohr, OFM,
founder and animator of the
Center for Action and Contemplation
whose commitment to and articulation
of Gospel values have so blessed
the Center in its early years.

Center for Action and Contemplation

VISION
We envision CAC as a faith alternative to the dominant consciousness, offering hope, inspiration and challenge to a despairing world.

PHILOSOPHY
We believe in:
A God who is RADICAL GRACE.
A humanity that is wounded but capable of transformation.
A society that is beyond the boundaries of race, nation, culture, gender, and religious differences.
A personhood with both rights and responsibilities.
Prayer and involvement with the issues of our time.
A simple, nonviolent life, rooted in the Gospels.
A never-ending need to be educated, converted to, and supported in these beliefs.
Our experience of truth based in the Judaeo-Christian tradition.

MISSION
We commit to:
Networking to promote a consistent ethic of life and the work of justice and peace.
Educating towards and living nonviolently, precariously, and contemplatively.
Actively engaging in transforming society from a faith perspective.
Collaborating with other organizations endorsing a similar vision and philosophy.

In this spirit, we invite you to join us ...

This is what Yahweh asks of you; only this:
to act justly,
to love tenderly,
and to walk humbly with your God.

Micah 6:8

Contents

Part II:

TO LOVE TENDERLY

Foreword

The Best Criticism of the Bad
Is the Practice of the Better

When we founded the Center for Action and Contemplation in 1987, need, call, and desire came together in almost perfect symmetry. Years later now, it still feels like grace—grace in action.

It was still the era of the Cold War. Sides were drawn and taken, but few were clearing middle ground. The Reagan illusion was obvious to most of the world, except to those comfortable with illusion in the U.S. hall of mirrors. A post-Christian era had turned most of academia and the media into expressing an attitude of benign neglect toward religion. The encyclical *Humanae Vitae*, with its prohibition of contraception, and the *Roe vs. Wade* decision for Americans led thoughtful people into tailspins with authority and institutions. The vacuum was often filled by the Religious Right, who appeared to be taking the moral high ground. The Left largely retreated from the public forum into private spiritualities.

In the Roman Catholic Church, a Polish pope was dividing the church too neatly between the teachers and the learners, when it was obvious even to humble people that the teachers had much to learn and the learners much to teach. Seventy percent of the Roman Catholic Church was now in the underdeveloped world, and new questions and perspectives were as certain as the dawn. No one had the need or the desire to take on the great institution anymore. Knowing that God and the Holy Spirit in history will "blow where they will" (John 3:8), many left the church. They could wait no longer. But some, whose sails were full, set their tack in a new but very old direction: toward communion. The polarities, the dualisms, the seeming opposites are not opposites at all but part of a hidden and rejected wholeness. The task of true religion is to rebind (in Latin, *re-ligio*) that which is torn apart by temperament, ignorance, and institutionalized evil. As Christians, we were driven and grounded by Jesus, "in whom all things can be held together . . .

and in whom all things are reconciled" (Col. 1:11,19)—even popes and presidents!

On a practical level we were convinced that praying and thinking are not mutually exclusive. Neither are praying and acting. With Ralph Waldo Emerson we wanted to shout to our country and our church, "Give us truths. We are tired of the surfaces!" We knew that mere information, the so-called knowledge explosion, actually tends to break things apart into competing ideologies. Wisdom, achieved only through contemplative seeing, puts things back together again. The most radical, political, and effective thing we could do for the world and the church was to teach contemplation: a way of seeing beyond the surfaces that fires one toward credible action.

Contemplation, in non-mystified language, is the ability to meet Reality in its most simple and direct form. When I let go of my judgments, my agenda, my tyrannical emotive life, my attachment to my positive or negative self-image, I am naked, poor, and ready for The Big Truths. Without some form of contemplative surrendering, I see little hope for breakthrough, for new ground, for moving beyond the hysterical ideologies of Left and Right, the small mind, and the clutching ego. Action without contemplation is the work of hamsters and gerbils. It gets you through the day, it gives you a temporary sense of movement, but the world is not made new by spinning wheels going nowhere. Yet even educated people seem content to stay in that place.

But religion has its own wheels: prayer wheels. We clergy love to keep them spinning too. Since Jeremiah's time, we have been shouting, "The sanctuary, the sanctuary, the sanctuary!" And God keeps telling us through the prophets, "Amend your behavior and your actions, and I will be with you in this place . . . if you treat each other fairly, if you do not exploit the stranger, the orphan and the widow, if you do not shed innocent blood, then I will be with you here in the sanctuary" (Jer. 7:3, 5–7).

These wheels are repeated in the secular realm by therapies disconnected to world therapy, by removing the soul from the *anima mundi* and refusing to recognize how these two things mirror each other. As James Hillman says, "By going inside (and remaining there!) we maintain the Cartesian split: the world out there is dead matter and the world inside me is living." It's bad psychology and it's surely bad religion, even though we have a lot of it. Maybe only "family systems therapy" is valid and all individual problems and hurts must be healed in context. Remember, the Bible only offered us salvation in the context of salvation *history*. Sin also is a part of a larger history of sin that we need to recognize and oppose. Pseudocontemplation wants to do inner, quiet, private work and avoid the practical order that teaches us how to sin and makes it profitable.

Contemplation without action is *certainly* not contemplation at all. Jesus seemed to think it might even be the greater danger: "If the light inside you is, in fact, darkness, what darkness that will be!" (Matt. 6:23). Concrete action in the world of relationships keeps us from a world of self-delusion about our own "enlightenment."

Corporate evil can only be confronted by corporate good. The isolated individual is a good starting point but becomes rather incapable as the struggle continues. In the 1970s and 1980s I was meeting many idealistic, dedicated Catholics on the road. They had made a retreat, been challenged by a sermon, and started a soup kitchen in Ohio or a battered women's shelter in Washington. Mature Christians were working for nuclear disarmament or going to jail for immigration rights. But often the very parish that had awakened them to the Gospel had no resources to educate, support, and empower them spiritually. Often, the present state in which they found themselves was worse than the first because they now felt let down by the church.

By the 1980s, many dioceses and parishes had formation programs for the in-house ministries of the church (religious educators, musicians, eucharistic ministers, administrators, and so forth). But there were few places for the burnt-out and burning out activists in the church. We were losing some of our brightest and our best to mere liberal or Leftist kinds of thinking. When failure, discouragement, persecution by friends and church showed themselves, there was no one there to tell them about the folly of the cross, the chemistry of forgiveness, and the descent into soul. The gospel had again failed to become real.

It is these folks to whom the Center for Action and Contemplation has been ministering through its seminars and internship program. It is these folks who have been reading *Radical Grace* through seven volumes and seven years. Here we gather some of the best from our circle of experienced travelers. Seldom will we give you clear answers or definitive directions, but we *will* make you at home in the world of soul. We *will* offer you what has always been offered us: a "free sample" of Spirit. A sample is all you need for a lifetime of driven desire, because the pattern is always the same:

> As above, so below,
> As the inner, so the outer,
> As the human body, so the Body of Christ,
> As the atom, so is the universe,
> As the human desire, so is God's desire.
> We need only put them together.

Richard Rohr, OFM
CAC Founder and Animator

Preface

The Center for Action and Contemplation was founded in 1987 when Fr. Richard Rohr, OFM, gathered a number of people intent on integrating contemplative spirituality and involvement in the pain and problems of our world.

From the Center's beginning, one of its most far-reaching ministries has been the publication of *Radical Grace,* a bimonthly newspaper currently reaching over five thousand people in the United States and twenty-four other countries. Through the years our writers have reflected on activism and the issues of our day, on contemplation and soul work, and on the integration of action and contemplation that is the CAC's primary goal.

That these articles have been well received has been affirmed again and again by notes from our readers, comments from program participants, and visitors to the Center—all grateful for their recognition that they are not alone, that the Center provides a vast informal network of people who share their faith, values, dreams, and commitment. It is our hope in offering this selection of *Radical Grace* articles that many others will be similarly inspired, challenged, and encouraged.

Radical Grace has been the work of many hands: Demetria Martinez, our first editor who is currently staff writer for the *National Catholic Reporter;* Pat Simmons, CAC codirector and coeditor from 1988 to 1993; Eileen Burke, former newspaper reporter and current coeditor; C. Rachael Howell, who does the newspaper art coordination and layout; Carole Wright, our typesetter; and all those writers who, whether or not their work appears in this book, have contributed so much. Special thanks to the CAC staff: codirector Wendy Corry, Hugh Doyle, Marie Nord, *Radical Grace* assistant managing editor Avis Crowe Vermilye, Jody Hart, Myrna Westberg, and the many volunteers who contribute so generously to the Center's daily life. Our gratitude to Teddy Carney who, from her California home, independently suggested the book at about the same time the idea surfaced at a staff meeting and who has devoted countless hours to the selection of articles. Finally, we thank Bob Heller of Crossroad for support and encouragement for this project.

For more information about the Center for Action and Contemplation and its programs, or for a free sample of a current issue of *Radical Grace,* contact us at:

Center for Action and Contemplation
P.O. Box 12464
Albuquerque NM 87195-2464
(505) 242-9588
(505) 242-9518 (FAX)

Christina Spahn
CAC Codirector,
Coeditor of Radical Grace

Part I

TO ACT
JUSTLY

When Charity Is Not Love

RICHARD ROHR, OFM

We must work to create a world in which it is easier for people to do good, said Peter Maurin. And that is our difficulty today. We are surrounded by good, well-meaning folks who are swept along in a stream of shallow options. Not only is the good made increasingly difficult to do, it is even increasingly difficult to recognize at all. It seems that affluence takes away the clear awareness of what is life and what is death. I do not think the rich are any more or less sinful than the simple and the poor, but they just have many more ways to call their sin virtue. There is a definite deadening of the awareness of true good and true evil. In its place, we have mostly opinionated folks and sentimental opinions at that. Is there any turning back (or forward!) to awareness?

I have found one fuzzy area that often needs to be clarified before spiritual conversion can take place: We have confused justice and charity. Charity was always considered the highest virtue and was popularly thought of as a kind of magnanimous and voluntary giving of ourselves, preferably for selfless motives. As long as we rose to this level on occasion, such as giving gifts at Christmas or baskets at Thanksgiving and occasional almsgiving, we could think of ourselves as charitable people who were operating at the highest level of virtue. The spiritual trap was that we always remained in charge; we decided who was worthy and unworthy of our love, and we garnered significant self-esteem as a byproduct. The question then becomes: Is this really virtue at all or actually an avoidance of the Divine Caritas? Is it any type of surrender or just another type of control? Are we instruments of God's love flowing into this world, or are we perhaps inhibiting that flow by our lack of true solidarity? Ordinarily, we wait for some onrush of warm, sad, or guilty feeling to drive us again to "an act of charity." What suffers in both giver and givee is the redemptive experience of true union and compassion. Some immediate needs might be met (and that's good), but the Lord and the great Good News are not well served. In other words, no new creation unfolds, no new peoplehood is formed, no healing grace is outpoured. It is just the same old system continued. Maybe that is why salvation history has proceeded at such a snail's pace among the comfortable: We have tried to be charitable without being just, we have tried to give without letting go, we have wanted to consider ourselves Christians while being only enlightened pagans.

What has been lacking is the virtue of justice. The Christian virtue of justice is indispensable to charity. Justice and charity are distinguishable but clearly inseparable in the teaching of the Doctors and the social encyclical letters of the Popes. The giving and caring spirit of charity both motivates and completes our sense of justice, but the virtue of charity cannot legitimately substitute for justice. Persons capable of doing justice are not justified in preferring to "do charity." Although this has clearly been taught on paper, I would say it is the great missing link in the practical preaching and lifestyle of the church. We have ignored the foundational obligation of justice in our works of charity and thus have ended up not even doing charity! For centuries we have been content to patch up holes temporarily (making ourselves feel benevolent) while in fact maintaining the legal and institutional structures that created the holes (making those at the bottom feel like victims). Now it has caught up with us in unimaginable poverty, dysfunction, alienation, and human abuse.

The question of basic social justice has been unasked and undemanded for so long—even by the redeemed society of the church—that when we ask it today we are considered to be troublesome, leftist, or dangerous. Even a bishop of the church like Dom Helder Camara of Brazil is forced to say, "As long as we feed the poor, they call us saints. But when we ask *why* there are poor, they call us communists." The questions of justice will always be subversive and countercultural to those who are enjoying the fruits of the system as it is. That is why Jesus' proclamation of the Kingdom is *good news* only for the poor (Luke 4:18). "You must not be surprised, brothers and sisters, that the world hates you" (1 John 3:13). What else could any self-maintaining system do? That is why the teachings of Jesus have put us on a collision course with the world that needs to divide us into those with the power and those without it. Instead, Jesus preaches a social order in which true charity is possible, a way of relating by which cooperation and community make sense. Jesus offers a world where all share the power of the Spirit "each according to his or her gift." And that "Spirit is given to each person for the sake of the common good" (1 Cor. 12:7). And that is the key to Christian community and Christian social justice. It is not a vision of totalitarian equality, nor is it capitalist competition (read: "domination of the fittest"), but a world in which cooperation, community, compassion, and the charity of Christ are paramount—and to which *all* other things are subservient.

Do we any longer believe this? Do we think it is a realistic political option? Is it even worth working for? Or should we head off to the desert? I'm afraid that we have too often prayed that the Kingdom *come*. We are trapped with an answer.

That kingdom reigns not just when the oppressed are liberated but even more when the oppressors are liberated from their insecurities and fears. It seems we are essentially involved in one another's conversion to justice and charity. We cannot hate, compete, compare, or dominate one another and still expect the new community of Christ to unfold. Our assurance that this is the Gospel is that God in Christ does *none* of these to us!

The whole struggling world is belatedly wrestling with these issues. People of good will on left or right, East or West, believer or agnostic are reaching beyond the dichotomies of this century. Perhaps none has expressed it more succinctly and even humorously than Jaime Cardinal Sin of Manila. To an American audience he said:

> "Strength without compassion is violence, compassion without justice is weakness, justice without love is totalitarianism, and charity without justice is baloney!"
> *Right on, Jaime!*

Both Sides of the Wall

RICHARD ROHR, OFM

*F*orty-three public addresses, five workshops, twenty-seven receptions or interviews, and thirty-one cities in thirty-four days. My European speaking tour was exhausting but also very rewarding and challenging.

Let me begin my summary reflections with my final journal entry: "Well, what did I learn and what did I give? The Europeans are definitely our roots and yet they are so different from us Americans: We are naive, and obviously so; they are cynical in a deep and not so obvious way. We are without real history; they are burdened down with it. We are into cheap grace; they are terrorized that there might not be any at all. The true and radical Gospel would go far and deep in these countries who are so tired of religion. Soft Catholic piety and hard Protestant headiness have given them many good reasons for boredom. They got as excited as twelve-year-olds at presentations of nonviolence, community, male spirituality, and contemplative emptiness.

"My first serious visit to an established socialist country was enlightening. The true price that the Eastern Europeans have paid was evident, not so much in the deterioration of the infrastructure, the limited goods, and omnipresent lines, but in the separation from the humanity and spirituality of the rest of the planet. Yet that very limitation has also caused many to go deeper, discovering what deserves to be discovered and forgetting what deserves to be forgotten. The Christians in Eastern Europe have a wisdom and depth that I do not see in Western Europeans.

"The most important gift I gave was undoubtedly the teaching on contemplation: 'the long, loving look at the Real.' This was truly revolutionary to many of them, yet was a clear return to the more ancient Catholic tradition they once knew so well: Julian of Norwich, Eckhart, Mechtild, Nicholas von Flue, and Hildegard, their holy ancestors. I am convinced that contemplation is the most radical thing that we can teach and live. What else will lead us beyond words, endless theories, and the prison of the private self? The first commandment of non-idolatry and the second of God as Holy Mystery are all that we can ever offer. "After too, too many words, now all ends in silence. Silence alone is broad enough and deep enough to encompass the Whole Mystery. All ends, and ends well, in silence" (Journal entry: March 26, 1990).

In both England and Germany, I was awed by the early arrival of my brother Franciscans within a few years after the death of Francis in 1226. In Canterbury, the ruins of Greyfriars still stand along a quiet stream. The Franciscans gathered the cream of the youth from Oxford and Cambridge. What Gospel did they live and preach and what longing led so many to this new form of religious life and commitment? In many Germanic cities, they still refer to the medieval Franciscan houses as the *Barfuss Kirche* (the church of the barefoot ones) or the Church of the Minorites. Could it have been their radical economics that inspired a new generation? Or was it their intense brotherhood? Will we rediscover such a Gospel in our lifetime?

They told me that before the East German Revolution in November 1989, the people were by and large for socialism. There was almost no dissent, only the prayer services for peace at St. Nikolai Church on Monday evenings. I spoke there at the final service before the giant demonstration in Leipzig's main square. Now, four months later, two-thirds of the people have left the party, police and teachers have changed their rhetoric and lost their credibility, and many of the lifetime party faithful have become cynical and embittered. I was told in Dresden that there is a high suicide rate among these groups. I wonder if most of us operate out of a kind of tactical truth. Or do we ask the question of truth at all? Maybe we are all just survivors and the pragmatic is really very understandable. It's probably why Jesus said so often, "When the Son of Man returns will he find any faith on earth?" (Luke 18:8). Whatever their politics or philosophy, I hope that the Eastern Europeans do not lose what they have that is good. They have learned to share and how to be happy with fewer goods and choices. Most would admit that their needs were well met. I guess that is why we call them the Second World. I worry that the overdeveloped First

World seems to be the reference point. Many understand, however, and they encouraged me to remind North Americans that the failure of Russian socialism *should not be interpreted as a victory of Western capitalism.*

Probably no country has experienced two such extremes in one lifetime as the East Germans. They went from right-wing Nazism to leftist socialism in the 1940s. Both systems (the extremes are amazingly alike!) told them what to do and taught them the way of fear. In the last days before the elections on March 18, 1990, there was an almost palpable anxiety everywhere. For the first time in their lives, many of them had a free choice. The implications of freedom were dawning on them, and they were not accustomed to it. I compared the people to teenagers in the scary summer before they enter high school: Can I compete? Will I make it? These people have had no expectation or training in choice, many areas of personal growth, the competitive job market, or Western thought in the last fifty years. After my first days, I realized it was necessary to simplify my theological and psychological vocabulary when I preached. The questions afterwards revealed that I was assuming far too much and going way over their heads. But their quickness, openness, and "humiliating humility" more than made up for their lack of familiarity with concepts readily understood elsewhere.

I was invited to speak to Catholic personnel and their families at an American base in West Germany. I was hosted by some enlightened North Americans who have seen beyond the myth and are ready to ask the next questions. Unfortunately, the powers that be are quickly trying to change the myth to justify a continued U.S. presence. Before we were "preserving the peace" and now we are "preserving stability." No one seems to be sure what that means, but two-million-dollar tanks drive up and down the highways and we continue to build new barracks, pave new roads, and generously pay the German farmers for the war games that destroy their fields and crops. It is difficult for many of the military personnel to cross over into the East and see that the "spies and communists" look just like us. I can see now why Jesus emphasized "leaving one's nets" to follow him. Job security embroils people in lifetime lies that are indeed very hard to expose. We North Americans really don't know how to live in peace or without enemies. Our economy, our self-image, our very psyche have lived in a triumphalist and paranoid stance for so long that it will be hard to change to a positive and creative mode.

But what can we do except continue to live and to *announce the alternative:* a new way of living based on faith instead of fear, peacemaking instead of money-making, community instead of competition. We are so addicted to the latter that it is hard to imagine the former. But Jesus is our imagination, and he told us that resurrection would come! The hope of this new era in Eastern Europe is another promise and guarantee that God has not given up on human history.

The Debt Crisis

PAT SIMMONS

*T*o set the stage: Of the five billion people on earth, 800 million or about one in five are chronically malnourished. In 1988, there were twelve to fourteen million refugees and fifty million migrant souls trying to escape war and famine. Forty thousand children die each day from causes that could have been prevented by inexpensive methods. According to UNICEF's *The Impact of the World Recession on Children,* there were definitive reverses in the 1980s for all major indicators of wellbeing for the old, sick, and children both in the newly industrialized and least developed nations. For example, in the thirty-seven poorest nations, spending on health care has been cut 50 percent and on education 25 percent. Servicing of the international debt is responsible for much of this setback.

How did it get so bad? In the early 1970s, oil producing and exporting countries deposited so much money that international banks were forced to look aggressively for borrowers in order to pay interest. They in turn bombarded finance ministers of less developed countries with loan offers. Especially hard pressured were countries such as Mexico and Brazil that were industrializing their economies.

The years between 1974 and 1979 saw economic growth accompanied by increasing indebtedness for third-world countries. The quality of life improved, and more people were reached by health services, primary education, and clean water. Improved nutrition was reflected in a decline of infant mortality and an increase in life expectancy. Dependence on the loans grew as countries experienced insufficient export revenue, rising costs of essential imports, and population growth.

Despite these measurable improvements, a large portion of the loan dollars were being returned to the First World through *first-world* employment and equipment purchases, availability of third-world raw materials for the *First World,* and access to new highways, communications and electricity built for the benefit of transnational corporations operating in the Third World. This helped offset recession in the industrialized countries. Use of the monies in the aforementioned ways were provisos of the loans and the Third World began to feel the crunch. When first-world inflation took off, the industrialized nations responded with higher interest rates, tight control of money supply, wage and price control, limitation of imports, and encouragement of exports. But no country can increase exports if all others are limiting imports, and the world economy moved closer to recession.

In 1982, Mexico announced to the world that it was unable to repay its debts on time and it was declaring a moratorium. After this announcement, renegotiated loan payments had even harsher conditions.

Adjustment measures for the Third World—that is, renegotiated debt terms—include the curbing of growth of public spending by a reduction of public subsidies, price increases for public services, restriction on money supplies, limitation of wage increases, and measures to increase exports and reduce imports. Devaluation of currency made imports of necessary supplies such as spare machinery parts and medicines unaffordable. The UNICEF study documents cuts in health care and food subsidies where the political cost was low while expenditures on defense and police remained stable. *Adjustment programs are directly responsible for the major decline in the quality of life for those least able to defend their interests.*

Another great tragedy is that many of the third-world loans favored the elite in some countries. Fortunes were salted away in tax-shelter countries rather than invested in the needs of the people.

Most of this third-world flight capital ended up in the United States, Great Britain, and Switzerland. In other countries, vast debts were incurred largely by repressive regimes that are no longer in power. Collectively, the Third World owes the astonishing sum of $1.2 trillion to first-world banks. Debt servicing consumes about one-third of the export revenue of the fifteen most indebted countries. The mountain of debt is growing and extensions of credit largely service existing debt.

In 1988, developing nations, despite desperate internal needs, transferred $43 billion to wealthy nations—a clear reversal from the 1970s. There is also a cutback on aid which some believe is caused by a "welfare mentality"—that is, some say the Third World has become a "scrounger." Global aid from the industrialized nations has stagnated at $32 billion a year or *the global equivalent of two weeks of military expenditure.*

For our part, the United States has insisted that debtor countries must sell government-owned enterprises to private investors to pay debts and has clearly been willing to save commercial banks at the expense of human well-being. Japanese aid to the Third World now outstrips ours, and we discourage further contributions as we fear giving Japan a greater say in running the international monetary groups in which we hold the power.

With the prevalence of unemployment and endemic hunger, third-world repayment of debts can only be achieved, if at all, at the cost of more hunger, increased impoverishment, and political instability. Debt crisis is not merely an economic and financial problem but relates to the very survival of large sections of populations or their right to develop. There is some question whether governments of some debtor countries could *survive* long enough to repay their debts.

For faith-based persons, it would seem that many important questions must be asked. How will adjustment programs to repay debt affect the poor in these countries? Should debtor countries be forced to cope indefinitely with debts incurred by past governments and the elite regardless of how corrupt? Should only the debts on money that *reached people* be repaid? If the loan money went to benefit transnational corporations operating in the Third World, is it fair for their struggling economies to carry the burden? Should debt servicing be postponed or debts forgiven for countries with critically weak economies? Are adjustment terms moral that continue to benefit the third-world elite despite the internal growing disparity between the rich and the poor in those countries?

I sometimes stare at a beautiful photograph of Earth, taken from a satellite, on my office wall and consider these words from Jacques Costeau as he commented on a similar satellite view:

> We are struck by the important differences between the way cartographers make our planet and the way it can be seen, given the perspective of the universe. There are no boundaries on real planet Earth. No United States, no Soviet Union, no China, Taiwan, East Germany or West. Rivers flow unimpeded across the swath of continents. The persistent tides—the pulse of the sea—do not discriminate; they push against all the varied shores on Earth.

Industrialized countries contain 23 percent of the world's population, less than one person in four, but control 80 percent of the world's goods. That leaves 20 percent for the other three-fourths of the world's population. The margin seems to be growing.

It would seem that faith-based persons need to view the debt crisis from an ethical dimension—to go beyond an approach or response that comes from enormous disparities of power and fixed boundaries separating us from them. Lord, when did I see you hungry?

A Prodigy in Rags

JERRY ORTIZ Y PINO

This article is reprinted from the December 4, 1991, Santa Fe Reporter.

*B*reakfast at the homeless shelter had ended, and much of the crowd of ragged, dispirited men and women had filtered out into the parking lot where those who had cigarettes were trying to avoid eye contact with those who didn't.

On cold winter Sundays, as many as two hundred people will show up for the hearty breakfast served by volunteer crews at this shelter. In the summer the crowd thins out, but we've never had fewer than 120 come in for the meal. A handful of street people stay afterward to clean up the dining area while we scrub the pots and pans and try to leave the kitchen in a semblance of order.

As the cleanup goes on, a few of our guests will hang around, chatting quietly or simply enjoying the hot coffee and relative comfort of the folding chairs. Some wait to talk with the chaplain, a woman who, incredibly, knows most of them by name. It's a time of calm after what is often a tumultuous mealtime.

Last month, as we were getting ready to close up the kitchen, a hauntingly beautiful rendition of Pachelbel's *Canon in D Major* suddenly filled the shelter. Then a Chopin sonata, some Brahms, a piece by Mozart—lovely music cascading from the corner of the main room where a battered upright piano had gathered dust for many months.

Oh, occasionally one of the shelter's clients would pound out a butchered version of "Heart and Soul" or even chopsticks on the instrument. And once a teenager from Mexico had silenced the crowd with a brief concert of mariachi standards. But the torrent of gorgeous music that showered us this morning was entirely different. This was a display of masterful talent, a skill that could only have come from years of disciplined practice. These were sounds made by a man in love with the music.

And these were sounds made by a tousle-haired young man wearing a filthy fatigue jacket, lacerated jeans, and scruffy tennis shoes. He kept his eyes squeezed tightly shut as he played and was oblivious to the effect his impromptu recital was having on the others in the room. He was alone with the beauty of the sounds he was so effortlessly pulling from the piano.

I don't know that young man's story. I would love to. I am curious about the circumstances that could have led such a prodigious talent to wind up on the streets of Albuquerque. A hundred scenarios suggest themselves. But, since I didn't ask, I don't know. And that's true for every homeless person in America today. They cannot be simply categorized, because they came to their extreme situations by a thousand routes. And until we learn to ask, we will continue to be misled by blanket statements about "the homeless."

But if we can't hope to speak with accuracy about such a diverse group when we use blanket phrases, we can do so much about society's response to burgeoning numbers of homeless, for that response is not at all diversified. We treat—and have consistently treated—the plight of the homeless as if it were a personal failure: What went wrong with them that they gave up?

But the more apt question, the one that leads somewhere, is: What are we as a people doing that is producing such a phenomenon? Here are a few of the changes that we've made in the United States in the last twenty-five years that have contributed to the population explosion on the streets. We didn't take these steps in order to create homelessness—but when the homeless began becoming impossible to avoid noticing, we weren't willing to change what we were doing. They became "unavoidable casualties" of our social policy.

What all these changes have in common is that they saved some group somewhere in the country some money. Think about this when you hear about "middle-class tax revolt" or when the wealthy complain about "throwing good money after bad" on welfare problems.

Change no. 1: We decided the War on Poverty was too expensive to wage.

Change no. 2: We decided that seriously disturbed people could be dealt with less expensively by turning them out of the public mental hospitals.

Change no. 3: We decided to let manufacturers shut down operations in this country and shift their plants to third-world nations.

Change no. 4: We inflated real estate values dizzyingly beyond the increases in wages.

Change no. 5: We have replaced menial jobs with automation.

Change no. 6: We engage in a policy on drug and alcohol abuse that emphasizes punishment over treatment.

And there are many others—each one a choice we made, each one a new spigot pouring additional thousands of previously marginal but surviving Americans into the streets.

Collectively, these choices have produced thousands of millionaires in the last ten years. For them, the "Land of Opportunity" never offered juicier pickings. But for the millions of homeless created by those same choices, the notion of "opportunity" is very hollow.

Exploring an Alternative: Priesthood and Marriage

CHRISTINA SPAHN

*I*n recent months I have attended two programs, a workshop and a retreat, led by former priests. In both cases the priests had recently married, and their wives were cofacilitators of the programs. Early on in their presentations, each couple briefly reflected on the life journeys that had led to their marriages and on the giftedness of these journeys. In neither account were bitterness or anger evident. Instead, very obvious parts of their histories were an in-touch-ness with their individual lives, a process of prayer and reflection open to God's Spirit, and a current peaceful integrity that was neither apologetic nor crusading.

For many years I have theoretically supported the option of a married priesthood. Meeting these two couples, experiencing the gifts of their ministries enhanced by their marriages, has transferred the issues out of my head and into my heart.

These real people, moved further into Christian maturity by the soul searching demanded in giving up their active priestly ministries, were characterized by all that one would wish in the priestly charism. It strikes me as immensely sad that there is presently no room for their priesthood in the church.

To say that I am *for* a married priesthood does not mean that I am *against* a celibate priesthood. What is important for both the celibate and the married person is that one can grow in love, can grow to the fullness of his or her maturity. For some this way is through a committed and life-embracing profession of celibacy. For such people, the emphasis needs to be not on what they have given up but on what they are given to. While a celibate relationship is different from a married relationship, the celibate is no less called to wholesome human intimacy. Unless the celibate's life is characterized by as much love, compassion, generosity of spirit, prayer-fulness, and commitment to ongoing conversion as can be expected of noncelibates, this person has failed life's project miserably.

To say that a celibate lifestyle has a definite and time-honored place in the church, however, does not negate the fact that it has been abused by the church. Celibacy, like marriage, demands growth. It is not static but process-oriented, necessitating the engagement of one's whole person. Through the ups and downs of the maturing process, the celibate becomes more whole, and his or her prayer, relationships, self-understanding, and ministry are positively affected.

For the person called to celibacy, this lifestyle is the way to God and to holiness. However, abuse has occurred in the assumption that all called to ordination are likewise called to celibacy. What happens to the person who is not so called? What happens to the person who perceives celibacy simply as a church discipline, imposed from the outside, that one must accept in order to be ordained? It is highly likely that such a person will never internalize and integrate the possibilities of his life. Not interiorly moved to pursue growth in celibacy and not legally free to explore a married lifestyle, this person can become fragmented and disengaged.

It is a tragedy of history that we have come to the present situation in the church; it is a tragedy of our time that we perpetuate it.

How did we arrive at the present situation in which marriage is honored as a sacrament, seen as a way to God, and denied to the ordained? The law of celibacy explicitly promulgated by the Second Lateran Council in 1139 was based on a negative understanding of sexuality. Influenced by Jewish tradition and the purity laws observed by pagan priests, fourth-century Christian priests were forbidden sexual intercourse the night before celebrating the Eucharist. Once eucharistic celebration became a daily occurrence, perpetual abstinence was the theoretical result—although it took several more centuries and church decrees for its full enforcement.

By the twelfth century, we had the obligation of priestly celibacy, founded on unhealthy attitudes toward sexuality and further boosted by the awareness that institutional life was far less complicated if church property was not subject to the inheritance claims of priests' children.

For the first time in canonical documents, Vatican II spoke of celibacy "for the sake of the kingdom." Faced with almost seven hundred years of imposed celibacy, the Second Vatican Counsel attempted to justify it, as Trent had earlier. However, while our theologies for both marriage and celibacy are improving, the old antisexual attitudes still seem to be in place. What else explains the fact that single men ordained to the permanent diaconate must promise celibacy prior to ordination and that married permanent deacons are not permitted to remarry if their present wife dies? What else explains the church's frequent head-in-the-sand posture in regard to the sexual practice of its clergy: heterosexual and homosexual involvement, pedophilia, and promiscuity (the promiscuous priest who can manage a low profile is dealt with more kindly than one who vows fidelity in marriage!)? What else explains the Vatican's apparent willingness to sacrifice our most central sacrament, Eucharist, to what, at one level, appears a rather arbitrary discipline (Throughout the centuries the Eastern church has continued to ordain both married and celibate men.)?

Permitting a married priesthood will not solve all priestly problems. Personal difficulties will still remain, and questions of authority, power, service, and relationship to the rest of the church will still need answers. Clerical marriage will not solve these and other problems, but for those called to it, it would provide a better place in which to explore them.

Given the fact that the Roman Catholic clergy throughout the world is aging and the church is growing, it is highly possible, despite present rhetoric to the contrary, that a married priesthood is not too far away. However, if a married priesthood in the Western church is reinstated simply as a pragmatic response to a can't-do-anything-else situation (another solution, ordaining women, is even more unthinkable!), much will be lost.

Far more hopeful and life-giving would be an affirmation of the gifts of both celibacy and marriage and an institutional recognition that the vocation of ordained service can be enfleshed within the life commitment of either. Such an affirmation would be consistent with the current positive theology of sexuality and marriage, explicitly putting that theology into practice. And such an affirmation, freely chosen and committed in expressing the complementariness of celibacy and marriage, would call the ordained and the church to greater maturity.

Mending the Breach:
Love and Power

RICHARD ROHR, OFM

*P*ower assumes that life is lived from the top down and from the outside in. It draws its strength from elites and enforcement. As such it is efficient, clean, practical, and works well on many short-term goals. The Gospel offers us the inefficient, not-so-clean, multilayered, long-haul way of love. Love is lived much more from the bottom up and from the inside out. It is easy to see why even the churches don't believe it. It does not give ego or institution any sense of control. Often it doesn't even "work."

Perhaps one way of stating the "spiritual emergency" that Catholic Christianity is facing today is that most of the present clergy and membership were trained from the top down and the outside in. Love was the message, but power/control was the method. Holiness was in great part defined as respect for outer mediating structures: the authorities that "knew," the rituals that were automatic (*ex opere operato*), the laws that kept you if you kept them, the Tradition that was supposed to be the unbroken consensus of many centuries and cultures. All this is wonderful and consoling if it were always true. I am convinced that the best that top-town Christianity can do is to get us off to a good start and keep us inside the ballpark, which isn't bad! But it is not close to satisfactory for the great struggles of faith that contemporary people face in family, morality, and society. It is a good runway, but it does not propel us into the realms of trial, mystery, sin, and sanctity. The burden of twentieth-century complex society!

The very depth and truth of the Gospel have led people to a more daring and necessary conclusion: Human life is best lived from the inside out and the bottom up. Now love is both the message and the method. Somehow "it is better to do wrong in your own way than to be right in someone else's," to quote Dostoevsky. Somehow my experience, my mistakes, my dead ends are not abhorrent to God but the very stuff of salvation. There is no other way to make sense out of the Bible or out of every human life that I have observed. Now we are secure enough to admit that there is just as much truth, maybe even more, inside our own journeys and in those at the bottom. So-called "tax collectors and prostitutes are making their way into the kingdom of God before you" (Matt. 21:31). Mature Christianity is perhaps when the inside meets the outside and the bottom is allowed to also teach the top. Sounds like pure Gospel to me.

Power and love are not mutually exclusive, but until I unlearn power in its usual form (and it is indeed an unlearning, which Christianity calls conversion), the mysterious event of love will not happen. If love does happen—a mystery, God-like—that we "fall" into and sometimes decide for, power emerges in a whole new form. This power is not only good but necessary and the conjugal partner of love. As Ernie Cortez of the Industrial Areas Foundation says, love without power is sentimentality and power without love is brutality. Love must be brought to earth; power must be lifted to the liberating heavens. Love relationships are necessary to make life bearable and beautiful; power relationships are necessary to get anything done.

What most people call power is just control. When I need to see that actions are done *my* way, I might have control over passing events, but that is not power in any full sense. Real persons of power can act, succeed, thrive—even when they do not have control. Power is the ability to act from the fullness of who I am, the capacity to establish and maintain a relationship with people and things, and the freedom to give myself away. If that sounds like religion's definition of a saint, you are right. Saints are the discoverers of that ideal blend between love and power.

Ironically, letting go of one's need for control has the potential to empower the whole group, staff, or family. If I do not need control to live and enjoy my relationships as they are, then everybody is called to a new level of trust and engagement. If the spaces between us are open and free, members can stop protecting and achieving and throw their hat into the great common ring. The movement from mere control to true power is probably the quintessential result of being loved. The obverse is also true: a controlled and controlling person is usually not being loved well at that point in life. The "holy madness" that Plato described as love makes control unnecessary, unattractive, and unreal. Once you have enjoyed real power, mere control is a counterfeit and a nuisance. People of power empower those around them. Controlling people control those around them. Which do you want to be? Which do you want to do?

St. Luke describes the gift of God's very self, the Holy Spirit, as a gift of "power." "You will receive power when the Holy Spirit comes on you" (Acts 1:8, 10:38; Luke 1:35, 24:49). It is strange, therefore, that Christians have had such a love-hate relationship with power. Clearly power must be something good, if God is power and God gives power. I suspect that we have rightly mistrusted power because we have seldom taken the longer Jesus path: the movement *through* control (all three temptations of Satan in the desert!) to true spiritual power.

Jesus named control and domination as the false form of power. "Among pagans it is the kings who lord it over them. . . . This must not happen with you!" (Luke 22:25–26). But then he continues by unapologetically contrasting it with true power: "You who stand faithfully with me through trials. . . . you will sit on thrones to judge the twelve tribes of Israel" (Luke 22:28,30). The power that Jesus trusts and offers is precisely the power that comes to us through the suffering of powerlessness, the power that is found when you have no control at all. The disciples' thrones are put in judgment over the false thrones of "those who make their authority felt." To make this concrete and contemporary: Mother Teresa has power, Cardinal Ratzinger has control. How wonderful when they occasionally come together in one person like Abraham Lincoln, John XXIII, or Dag Hammerskjöld. Love is the bridge. One cannot exercise control in the true form of power except through love. It is so rarely achieved that Jesus seems to warn his followers against ever seeking or exercising dominative power. Francis of Assisi teaches his followers the same. The Mennonites and the Amish at least tried noncooperation and nonparticipation in false power. After Constantine invited us into the power class in 313 A.D. much of the rest of Christianity has been unable to see the problem. Thus we have lived with centuries of 1) sanctified control (sacred law and clergy), 2) projected control (giving human laws divine authority), 3) disguised control ("I'm just enforcing what God has commanded"), 4) denied control (benevolent monarchs and bureaucracies), and 5) alliances with control (supporting governments who would protect our privileges, and police who do the controlling for us). And all in the name of the Jesus-Teacher who told us to do it differently! I am convinced that true spirituality is mediated through persons, images, rituals, and writings—but it does not really take a lot of middle management beyond that. I fear that we have been much more invested in Churchianity than committed to the Jesus Movement.

Jesus believes that *love will always rise from the dead*, good is more powerful than evil, and his Father will prove this once and for all in his human body. Until we know that in our bones, until we risk it in our actions, until we base our life's choices on such awesome trust, "all our preaching is useless and all our believing is in vain" (I Cor. 15:14). The mystery of the death and resurrection of Christ tells us that it is finally a Benevolent Universe, God is on our side, we belong here, and there is no basis for existential fear. We no longer need to control, because something much better is already in the works. The Easter Mystery says that the true apocalyptic message is not "The end is near!" but "The beginning is always happening!" Power cannot see that. Love can see nothing else.

Why Deterrence Is Death

RICHARD ROHR, OFM

*A*s far as the human soul is concerned, and that's our business, nuclear weaponry and nuclear deterrence are myths of immense illusion and regression. Insofar as we capitulate to their false promises of security, individual persons and our culture will surely not progress to deeper levels of spirituality or consciousness. The nuclear myth gets us off almost all the hooks that the Divine Fisherman uses: our powerlessness, our essential insecurity, the desire to give one's life for something bigger than oneself, our fear of death, our capacity for faith, trust, and forgiveness, our restless hearts that long to be united.

Once we squelch all of this energy in the name of hard-headed intellect and will, three not-so-obvious demons will move in to take the place of Spirit: *expedience, law, and propriety.* I see many well-meaning believers living out of this American ethic and honestly not aware that they have abandoned the meat and marrow of the Gospel and put their hope in reasonableness and "enlightened" self-interest. Such "wisdom" even seems to make sense to many of the bishops, but it is not pure Gospel. It's feel-good, intelligent, practical civil religion. And we have grown used to it for so long that we think it is the teaching of Jesus. The three demons have done a good job of disguise. As demons are wont to do, they have made evil look like virtue.

Let's take *expedience.* It's about all you have if you have not formed and developed your conscience. It is an early stage of moral development, but it finds no support in the words of Jesus. "Even the tax collectors do as much, do they not? . . . Even the pagans do as much, do they not?" (Mátt. 5:46, 47). It is reflected in the moral Christian parent who is righteously concerned about the evils of premarital sex but, when questioned, reveals that the real concern is for family embarrassment, future marriage possibilities, schooling, career, and who will pay for it. Reasonable and under-standable concerns, but hardly dealing with real moral evil or Christian spirituality. We have padded and protected our people at this level for so long that many of them seem incapable of recog-nizing, much less responding to, the real goods and evils that con-front our age.

This brings us to the second false savior: *law.* Now I know that most folks think this is what religion is all about: law and order, control, doing what you're told, obeying commandments, and win-ning divine assurances. Paul clearly taught the opposite in the whole book of Romans, "a person is justified by faith and not by doing works prescribed by the law" (3:28). Or even better, "If the world is only to be inherited by those who submit to the law, then faith is pointless and the promise worth nothing" (4:14). Whew! That's good to know!

Unfortunately, most religious people don't. The church got itself into the business (and I do mean business) of issuing salvation passes for good behavior instead of doing what Jesus did: proclaiming and living the new reality based on Truth, which he called the Reign or Kingdom of God. Law is a nice way to feel good about yourself without actually being good, a fine way to control the troops and keep those young girls from getting pregnant, an excellent way to satisfy that urge that seems to afflict religious people without actually surrendering to God, to love, or to Life itself. Law will always take over when there is no real wrestling with the angels of Yahweh who always dislocate our hip bones so we can't walk on our own (Gen. 32:25). Law will always dominate people who have not experienced that the Spirit blows where it pleases (John 3:8) and cannot be controlled by our righteousness. Law is the false promise for those who control life from their heads, those who are afraid to listen anew right now, those who substitute principles for prayer and people. As St. Thomas More said, there is no better place to hide than "behind the thickets of the law." And he was a lawyer!

Sadly, strangely, obedience to "laws" is one of the safest places to avoid God, to avoid conversion, to avoid the spontaneous movement of the Spirit. I remember the first time I was arrested in Washington for protesting nuclear weapons production. The nastiest letters I received were from good Catholic lawyers who seemed to have made an idol of civil law. That's what happens when we become specialists and even experts in one area, while allowing our spiritual and theological education to remain at the level of grade school. Our country is filled with such Christians. Law is not adequate to name or support the full work of the Spirit. Sometimes it even opposes it. Why else do you suppose Jesus warned us about persecution from church and state? Why do you think Jesus himself was killed by the "good" law-abiding people?

The message is shouting at us: "The kingdom of God does not mean eating or drinking this or that, it means justice and peace and joy brought by the Holy Spirit" (Rom. 14:17).

And finally *propriety*. Being nice and proper like everybody else on the block seems always to have been a substitute for real conversion. Middle-class religion loves to bless and baptize "the way everybody thinks." It ends up making the Great Commandment and the Sermon on the Mount into a tidy lesson from Miss Manners. And the poor remain oppressed, the hungry unfed, the illusions maintained, the lie retold, "gnats strained out while camels are swallowed" (Matt. 23:24), and the human spirit remains without compassion—among nice, proper, churchgoing folks. Self-serving behavior has taken the place of other-serving love. So what does all of this have to do with nuclear bombs and nuclear deterrence? I am convinced that nuclear war is a spiritual problem. It is based on subtle but utterly devious perceptions of the human condition. The way out will depend on spiritual conversion, not theorizing or proving. Our job is first of all to convert the world, but to call the church to be the church (*ek-klesis* = the called-out ones). Pragmatism, law, and collective thinking are the demons that seem to be blocking the children of light from recognizing the full power of the Gospel. We need to be converted to our own Master and Lord before we can expect the world to understand. "Yet if the light inside you is darkness, what darkness that will be!" (Matt. 6:23). Our demons are legion and angelically costumed, while we aim our righteous sights on the obvious evils of the world.

Why is it that good Catholic children were universally taught that the famous sixth and ninth commandments "admitted of no parvity of matter" (in other words, it was *always in all circumstances bad bad!*) while the not-so-important fifth commandment ("Thou shalt not kill!") was routinely ignored by Catholic princes and Catholic prelates when it served their purposes of power and control. Come on! No wonder we have lost moral credibility with much of Western civilization. Such self-serving dishonesty is not even worth arguing against. We have trifled with true moral evil for so long while piously confessing liturgical failures as "mortal sin" that we seem no longer capable of recognizing the sin that truly does us in and hardens the heart and spirit. We have been on the side of power, collective thinking, and money for so many centuries that it is very difficult for many Christians to take again the side of Jesus and his extraordinary announcement of a New Reality.

We are still content to be apologists for the old reality, which in this case becomes the cold war, the military-industrial complex, the economy of the good old U.S.A. (apparently the first fruits of the coming of the Kingdom), and the prestige and respectability of the American Roman Catholic Church. We are still too anxious to appear as intelligent dialogical partners with the powers that be, so afraid to be accused of fanaticism or prophetism, that we end up providing no alternative to the system beyond questions and verbiage and papers that unfortunately very few people read. I know that we have had no training or encouragement in the prophetic charism. It is a lost gift except in the area of private morality. We are accustomed to forming teachers, pastors, administrators, and even apostles and healers, but the highly listed charism of prophecy (Eph. 4:11) is still scary, foreign and thought to be unnecessary by churches that have bought the system. Fortunately, we are again discovering the older and biblical notion of social and structural sin ("the sin of the world" that John the Baptist points out [John 1:29]). Pope John Paul II speaks of it in his hard-hitting encyclical *Solicitudo Rei Socialis.* His critical analysis of both Western capitalism and totalitarian communism shows a courage and prophetic leadership that we need from our American bishops in confronting the myth of deterrence and nuclear superiority.

Yes, people and nation-states have a right to safety and security; a certain degree of it is necessary for psychological, economic, and human growth. But that is quite different from the overarching and overbearing need that now seems to dominate all other human concerns. What allows us to think that food, housing, education, welfare, ecology, medicine, aesthetics, the animal and plant world, wisdom, family, and holiness are all supposed to be put on hold until American people can feel absolutely secure and victorious? No beings on this planet since the beginning of time have had the right to such security. But we have the money and the necessary mythology ("making the world safe for democracy," "the protectors of Western civilization," "the keepers of the faith," and so forth) to try to secure ourselves against all competitors.

It is spiritually destructive for the individual—"whoever wants to save his or her life will lose it" (Matt. 16:25)—and it is equally destructive for the collective. Until Catholicism recovers its great medieval synthesis, until it again sees itself as preaching the Gospel to the *nations* (Matt. 28:19), until it again acts as the corporate conscience and not just the comforter of private lives, we will surely continue to lose our moral credibility and moral leadership.

American bishops, our teachers and overseers, we ask you to pray, to reread the sermons of Jesus, to follow the prophetic leadership of the bishop of Rome. As many have said, the social encyclicals are still the best kept secret in the church! We ask you firmly and courageously to condemn the American myth of nuclear deterrence before we have lost both our planet and our spiritual soul.

One Man's Journey: Hearing The Prophets

JACK TISCHHAUSER

*P*eople who first hear the prophets are key to the work of the prophets. People who hear are people who listen. To hear, one must be quiet and one must not be caught up and absorbed in the precepts of one's culture. These people often share some of the fate of the prophets themselves. When the prophets speak, not only are most of the people absorbed in their own pursuits, but also often what the prophet is saying threatens those very activities. This, of course, is why the people don't want to listen to the prophets but want to silence them. Sadly, I have not been one of those who hear prophets.

When I was growing up, war was threatening, and World War II started when I was in my teens. It was an accepted part of our culture. There were times, however, in the clarity and innocence of childhood, when I thought objectively about war, and it seemed inconceivable to me that a country could focus all of its attention and energy on killing the people of another country. Nonetheless, I wanted to "serve my country" and I joined the Marines as soon as I could. Luckily, I was never in combat. After I graduated from college I went to work for Sandia Corporation. With World War II of such recent memory and the Korean war starting, there was just no question about the acceptability of making nuclear weapons. We were in the height of the cold war with Russia and in the aftermath of the Rosenberg spy scandal. We *had* to make weapons to keep ahead of the Russians. There were no prophets saying *no*. We had just finished a war in which destroying a city full of civilians in order to demoralize the enemy was a standard tactic. No one, including the church in America, spoke out against it.

My concern was to get an interesting job and to make a living for my growing family, which was already at two children when I finished college. As time went by, the prophets began to speak. A few, who were considered the lunatic fringe, began to oppose nuclear weapons. Most of us reacted with anger. "Why don't those leftist pinkos talk to the Russians about nuclear weapons?" Still, there were times even then, when in an introspective mood I wondered if I shouldn't spend my life and my professional career in something more constructive for the human race than building weapons of enormous destruction. I wondered if that was the legacy I wanted to leave. Even so, I didn't think it was wrong to build them—someone had to do it. I just didn't know if it should be me. However, it became more and more difficult to leave Sandia. I had seven children and had moved into management. I was making a good living. My job, which involved large computers, was interesting and exciting. I was assimilated into Sandia.

Then came the Vietnam war, and soon there were prophets to speak against it. Again, at first we didn't hear them. Then the process of the spreading of truth began. This truth spread more quickly than most, probably because it was having such a perceptible impact on people's lives. My first reaction to the Vietnam war was based on the naive assumption that I had always held, that those in government who made such decisions had access to much more information than I—and who was I to question it? But slowly my view began to change. During this process, I remember vividly getting a glimpse into what prophets must feel. My friend, Turk Levy, who had always been active politically and who also worked at Sandia, asked me to sign a petition against the Vietnam war. Although I was beginning to think the war was wrong, I remember my stark fear, at the prospect of signing that petition, of the repercussions on my position at Sandia. Once again, I failed to follow the prophets. I made a lame excuse about not being completely convinced, so that I wouldn't have to sign it. Of course I was eventually convinced that the war was wrong, but by then this was becoming the majority opinion in the country.

The Vietnam war had one good effect. The notion that our government had information that we didn't have and could be trusted to do what was right was demolished. As time went on, when I reflected on the question of the morality of nuclear weapons, I no longer felt hostile to those who were opposed to them. But I always came to the conclusion that we could not be defenseless and that deterrence was actually the only practical way to prevent a nuclear holocaust. Still, when I saw demonstrators at the gates of Kirtland, I felt admiration for their courage and conviction rather than hostility. I also felt a vague embarrassment as I drove past them. Perhaps deep in my subconscious I realized that I was sticking to the safety of the majority and rejecting the prophets. Those times often stirred me again to think about the question. I had admiration for the ideal of nonviolence but did not see how one could impose it on anyone but oneself. In my mind, to eliminate nuclear weapons, or even stop our development of them, would place us at the mercy of a brutal and ruthless enemy. In effect, we would be imposing the consequences of nonviolence on everyone.

In the last few years (since my marriage to Kathleen), I have been working seriously toward developing my relationship with God. As I came to know Jesus better, it became more and more clear that his message was completely incompatible with the activity with which I was associated. Our government is piling up nuclear weapons that can destroy the earth a thousand times over— far beyond what might be needed for simple deterrence. Furthermore, it became clear that enormous resources are being used for this that are desperately needed for the kind of things that *would* be compatible with Jesus' message.

The voices have become louder, and perhaps I am listening a little better; but I finally heard the prophets and decided that I no longer want to be associated with the business of making nuclear weapons. The final breakthrough came when I attended a workshop on nonviolence by Fr. Charles McCarthy in which he very forcefully brought home Christ's words on the last judgment, as stated in Matthew 25. Characteristically, I have been more like the apostles at the crucifixion, following at a safe distance, rather than being a bold witness for the prophets. I did not make a dramatic resignation but took an early retirement. Perhaps I can somewhat rationalize this action by the fact that the conviction came slowly rather than with dramatic suddenness.

After I announced my retirement, but before my termination date, the Lord, in his goodness, seems to have given me a confirmation. As I was taking a run across the mesa one day, I came across a Bible lying in the path. It was open to the first page of Matthew 25. As I grow in my spiritual walk and my relationship with God, perhaps I can become quiet enough and open enough to God's spirit that I will readily be able to hear the prophets.

A Wedding Garment and a Hair Shirt: Keeping Both on Hand

LINDA HARDY

*A*s I was leaving the Center the night of the dialogue with the Kirtland and Sandia folks, I noticed new issues of *Radical Grace* sitting in stacks by the doorway. In the prophetic voice of John the Baptist, the Center's patron, headlines proclaimed Why Deterrence Is Death.

I couldn't help smiling because I had just left a room in which the man who had written that story was passing out cheese and crackers to people who designed and perfected the weapons of deterrence.

But it struck me that there was no contradiction here, just the passing from one mode of being to another, a participation in the rhythm of life that dictates a time to speak and a time to listen, a time to rebuke and a time to affirm. That night I saw it as a time for a hair shirt and a time for a wedding garment.

I grew up in a family that was long on parties and short on prophets, so I'm always glad to hear that the Kingdom of God is like a wedding feast. What was alien to me growing up was the strange, wild figure of John the Baptist going off into the desert to eat locusts and wild honey. If they talked about him in church, I don't remember it (I probably tuned it out), and it took me a while to realize I'd only gotten half the story—the wedding feast without the prophets; or as Fr. Richard said at the Center's dedication, "Jesus loves you" without "Jesus wants you to be just."

I still love the wedding as an image of the kingdom because of what it celebrates—human complementarity—and because of the generous, inclusive spirit in which it is usually celebrated, in traditional cultures, at least. I can't imagine peasants anywhere in the world preparing for a wedding by poring over a guest list and deciding whom to scratch out. My hunch is that everybody who gets a whiff of the roasting pig gets to come.

The trouble with the wedding-feast theology that I grew up on (which says let's have the party without the prophet) is that it is espoused by people who have their plates piled high with roast pork and not by the people standing around empty-handed. And as long as there are people standing around empty-handed, there will be parties that get disrupted by prophets in one form or another.

I remember listening from the kitchen during a dinner party given by my parents in the fifties. All of a sudden, what had been pleasant conversation turned loud and contentious. I heard "Faubus" and "Little Rock" and finally my father's voice silencing the others.

"I'll tell you this," he said, spacing out his words for emphasis, "Nature . . . doesn't frown . . . on the union."

It was his way of saying that if integration led to intermarriage, as the guests feared, the human race would survive and might even take an evolutionary step up.

Glasses came down hard on the table and chairs were pushed away abruptly as the guests left in anger. The party was over.

Jesus ruined a dinner party, too, when he lit into the Pharisees for their hypocrisy, for tithing mint and rue and neglecting justice and the love of God. In neither case would politeness have redeemed the situation. When the harsh, divisive word of truth is called for, it has to be spoken. The abscess has to be lanced before it can heal.

A true feast is never a cover-up, a place to pretend all is well when it isn't. Given the state of the world, then, should we fast until things improve?

No. Because it is the nature of God to prepare us a feast in the midst of our enemies, to anoint us with oil, to fill our cup until it runs over.

The essence of a feast is this fullness to overflowing—not with food or wine, but with the spirit that says it is good just to be, and to be together. But when the spirit becomes exclusionary, celebrating not the goodness of being but the goodness of being rich or smart or miserable together, it may be a party, but it's not a feast.

Cana, I suspect, was a feast. I imagine Mary taking it all in—the brilliantly lit room, the festive wedding clothes, the heady air of expectancy—and knowing, "This is the time. This is the place." Jesus himself, after his initial hesitancy, may have sensed the ripeness of the moment as he saw his neighbors feasting in—and on—the fullness of their tradition, participating in prescribed rituals not as a burden but as an elaboration of their joy—because it was here, amid the talk and laughter and self-forgetfulness of his neighbors, that he chose to show us how the water of our humanity, in his hands, becomes the wine of the Kingdom. To be tasted now, since the Kingdom, after all, is among us—times like these, I'm tempted to add.

But immediately after this affirmation of his culture's rituals—where he could see that they clearly served the purpose for which they were intended, to keep Jews mindful of their covenant with God—we see him driving the money changers out of the temple, addressing that part of his culture which was untrue to itself.

He was able to slip out of a wedding garment and into a hair shirt (shorthand for the role of the prophet) because he wasn't enamored of either role. As an integrated person, he had the freedom to respond to the needs of the situation instead of the needs of his own psyche.

I would like to believe that we could all become that flexible. In the meantime, though, it appears that some people by temperament or circumstance end up being the full-time prophets and others the caterers at the feast. I'm hoping that if we can't switch roles, at least we can learn when it's time to defer to the other, when it's time to celebrate community—and everyone's right to be without being right—and when it's time to point out that however cozy it is in here, folks, Lazarus is at the gate.

You don't have to say that too many times before you end up at the gate yourself. And this may be the point at which you realize why the prophet lives on locusts and wild honey. When you're that far down on the food chain you can say anything you want because you've got nothing to lose. Except one thing—your humanity: a wholeness and humility that is greater than any role, no matter how worthy.

To put it another way, when the hair shirt starts to feel good, it's probably time to trade it in for a wedding garment. A wedding garment, you'll remember, is what you had to wear to a wedding feast. But it wasn't meant to exclude anyone, since it was easily obtained. To me it's a good symbol of a willingness to drop our private agenda and enter into a spirit of community with people who may not share our zeal for their conversion.

That's sometimes hard for prophets to do. Prophets often think, "If I'm not saving the world, what am I doing?", which is a question that a good party can answer. How? By giving them an experience of life that is not a contest between good and evil.

The person I know who could do this best was my Aunt Mercedes. Born in Nicaragua and married to an American, she was widowed at thirty-two and went back to nursing school to support her six children. Completely without artifice, she was the most beautiful woman I knew. Whenever I tried to imagine Mary, I saw Mercedes.

I said she had six children, but I was so often with them that she learned to count seven heads in the car before pulling out of the driveway. And we all pulled out into the mainstream of life just as the hippie parade was going by, which we joined and rerouted through her living room.

But it was hard to pass through Mercedes's living room and not want to stay for a while. The house itself was old and comfortable—a melange of hand-me-down furniture and the exuberant art of adolescents. And there was Mercedes herself, moving around the kitchen with that easy way of hers, not cooking huge quantities of food but somehow always having a little something on the stove for anyone who dropped by at mealtime.

Although a lot of teenagers who were alienated from their own parents felt at ease with Mercedes, she was not one of those people who pride themselves on "understanding youth," relishing the role of advisor and confidant. When things got too crazy she'd retire to her room, where a rosary and a picture of the Sacred Heart hung on the wall and "The Imitation of Christ" was near her bed.

The parties I remember best came during the turbulent, polarizing years of the 60s and 70s, when people who would have had nothing to do with each other any place else came together easily in the golden lamplight of her living room.

These parties started out as family gatherings, but as we started inviting friends, and then friends of friends, we just lost track. But

I know that you had to cast a wide net over San Antonio, Texas (and a big chunk of the world) to come up with the people you'd meet at Mercedes's house—a group of high school boys who improvised with the clarinet, piano, and guitar, and their friend Florence, who did interpretive dancing; a Mexican priest who sang for us; a beefy recruit from Fort Sam Houston; a Chicana activist; two Sikhs who spent six weeks at Mercedes's house; a genteel woman who lectured on salvation history in Catholic schools and her husband, the president of a local brewery; an older black woman who worked as a cook in a nursing home; a skinny kid who looked like he needed more food and less marijuana; some elderly relatives up from Central America for cataract surgery; a young woman recovering from mental illness who was content just to sit on the couch and watch. All of these were in addition to our own family, which was a mixed bag in itself.

You might think that conversation among such disparate types would have to remain superficially polite to avoid getting hostile. But that wasn't the case. I remember moments of real connectedness between people who in any other setting would have been downright surly to each other or, more likely, would have averted their eyes.

It worked because we were all wearing the wedding garments that Mercedes provided by her very presence, wedding garments that allowed us, emotionally speaking, to disrobe, disarm, and put on a larger identity.

I remember one man who slipped in without a wedding garment. He told Mercedes that her traditional morality was responsible for a lot of screwed-up women he'd met lately.

Mercedes smiled. "Oh?"

I saw him later in the kitchen scraping the last bit of *arroz con pollo* onto his plate and then settling down in a chair near the piano where my father was playing the Tennessee Waltz. He stayed later than anyone else.

It was hard to be in Mercedes's house for very long without surrendering to the alchemy of her living room, exchanging a role and an opinion for the richness of being fully human, at least for an evening. In her home there were no stereotypes. Everyone had a face, a voice, a way of laughing or just sitting on the arm of a chair—a personal radiance.

So that's why I was smiling when I left the Center the night of the dialogue. I was glad to know that the people here could wear wedding garments as easily as hair shirts. And I was happy to have found, in a school for prophets, of all places, the genial spirit of Mercedes's house.

If the Sewers . . .

SUE BROWN

*A*n old friend asked recently if I would be willing to go back to Haiti as part of a fact-finding team for CPT (Christian Peacekeeping Team). As I've thought about and meditated on this request, I am overcome by memories of Haiti when things were "normal." The effect of the U.S. embargo and the one in Iraq has been just to make the "normal" horrid problems more widespread. Now, instead of the occasional person dipping water out of the sewer, there are many. With an embargo, even the sewers may run dry.

As a North American, I had never thought about the *gift* of water except during my lazy midwest summers when rain was necessary for the farms and gardens to flourish. As I became a more "educated" urban-dweller, water became just something I could purchase in bottles with a little carbonation or another bill to be paid along with those for sewage and garbage services.

Then, in 1974, we moved to Gde Riviére du Nord, Haiti. The town of six thousand was along an innocent-looking river that carried the wash water and excrement for an area of 100,000 people down to the sea. In Haiti, the common wisdom is that if the water is moving, you can drink it. My North American problem-solving sprang forth: "I'll just teach people to boil the water so it will be OK to drink," until I realized that firewood was scarce.

Mennonite volunteers who had gone before us had approached the problem by capping springs in the nearby mountains to pipe water into the town. By the time we arrived, only one spigot was working. I have had memories of rising at 3 a.m. to haul our water before the masses of people got to the spigot and the daily fights for a place in line broke out. There was a high cost to preventive medicine!

But most people didn't line up for water. They drank from the river. It didn't take a microscope to see the excrement flowing in it as it ran through the town. I'd say to our sons who swam in the river, "I'd rather you not do that." They would reply, "Mom, how dumb do you think we are? We always swim with our mouths shut!" But the river was the social spot where kids gathered to swim, while their mothers exchanged news as they washed clothes and laid them on rocks to dry. And the majority of people drank the river water, swam in it, and bathed in it. Your standards change when it is hot and there is no place other than open sewers called rivers. Thirst is overwhelming.

At one time in Haiti I was assigned to a beautiful, U.S.-aid-built hospital in a town of four hundred people. It had eighteen beds, three open courtyards, eight flush toilets and *no* water.

As our years of living in Haiti stretched on, I wandered through various neighborhoods and watched people dip water out of running sewers or ravines. I'd just shake my head and think of our modern microbiology language which describes bacteria in the laboratory situation as "too numerous to count." It seemed to me that people were also too numerous, to count politically as they daily drank a little death in the guise of life-giving water.

The hospital was "run" by a couple of ladies who walked half a mile out of town each day and dipped "running" water out of the creek. We tried to "hospitalize" most people at home where it was better for their health. We even arranged for town families who had a little extra space to take in sick strangers so at least they could get water, food, and a bath, as the local people knew where and how to find water.

Another time I lived in Port-au-Prince for four months. The lack of water became even more personally scary because there wasn't a nearby river or spring. The city water depended on where those without water had found an exposed city pipe to break. When that happened, which was frequently, the poor would have water and the rich homes wouldn't. Then the city workers would repair the pipe, cover it up, and everyone would wait for the cycle to begin again. There was also a reservoir for rainwater on the property we rented. But as always in Haiti, there were additional pipes leading out and into the ravine behind the house where countless poor people had access to *my* water. I am embarrassed to recall how irate I would get watching the level of *my* water in the reservoir go down because they were taking it. Daily I'd anxiously check the level, worrying that maybe tomorrow the water would be gone. In time of scarcity, my true colors came out.

I became aware that the image of water is powerfully present through both the Old and the New Testaments. Biblical people knew at a deep and emotional level what water meant. The Bible has more than twice as many references to water and thirst as to food and hunger.

> O God, you are my God, I seek you early with a heart that thirsts for you and a body wasted with longing for you, like a dry and thirsty land that has no water. (Ps. 63:1)

The psalmist's imagery was not wasted on a biblical people, nor is it wasted today on the majority of Earth's people. They know what thirst means. All during the Persian Gulf War, I could feel the horror of a desert people without water. The lucky 100,000 were killed by our bombs while the rest of the population has to struggle on, not only without food and medical supplies but most desperately without adequate or reliable water.

Water inspired one of the most profound spiritual experiences of my life. In order to reduce diarrhea, hepatitis, and typhoid, we began capping springs anywhere in a twenty-mile radius. No trickle of water was too insignificant for us to teach the community to cap. Capping begins by digging back through a hillside. Dirt and rocks tumble down while you dig. Ultimately you come to the place where pure water bubbles up through rock. It just bubbles and bubbles, never stopping, true in its faithfulness.

> The wretched and the poor look for water and find none, their tongues are parched and thirst; but I, the Lord, will give them an answer, I, the God of Israel will not forsake them. (Is. 41:17)

No, I don't need to go back to Haiti or go to Iraq just now. I can see and feel it all too deeply. What I need to do now is to let the horror again flood my consciousness. If the sewers are running dry, there will be no place to drink. . . .

Love and Murder

MIKE ROCHE

I spent some time in India last summer studying and trying to practice nonviolence. When I returned to South Dakota, I found the state entangled in a death penalty debate incited by the trial, conviction, and death sentencing of Donald Moeller for the rape and murder of nine-year-old Rebecca O'Connell. The case is controversial not only because of the largely circumstantial nature of the state's case, but also because, if he is executed, Donald Moeller will be the first defendant to receive the death penalty in South Dakota since 1947. After the verdict, I wrote the following letter to the editor of the major newspaper in the state:

> Some years ago when the South Dakota legislature was considering whether to reinstate the death penalty, I went to Pierre to testify against such a decision. I suggested that the legislators should "beware of the terrible simplifiers" on either side of the capital punishment question, and I spoke with them at length about the tremendously complex legal, social, and moral issues that surround the debate. I also explained to them why my own analysis of these complicated issues led me to take a tentative position against the death penalty. The legislature voted to reinstate capital punishment.
>
> I'm not so tentative or sophisticated anymore. These days I can still appreciate the complexity of the death penalty debate at some abstract, intellectual level, but the more I see of Rebecca and Donald the more my heart comes to center on only one question—are we human beings as a species the flower of the evolutionary process or a fatal germ? If Donald Moeller did what he was found guilty of doing to Becky O'Connell, he was acting out of that place within him where the most wicked, ugly, and evil qualities of humankind reside.
>
> If we kill him for what he may have done to her are we not acting out of that same place? The question I wonder about

most these days is whether we can be strong enough, I could say "good" enough, to break the cycles of violence that seem so entrenched in our lives and our world and somehow affirm the higher qualities of love, mercy, and forgiveness.

As I look around the world and at the trials in my own life, I can see that absorbing the suffering like this and refusing to pass violence along may be the hardest thing in the world to do. Sometimes I don't think we have it in us.

Then I look at the lives of the great moral figures of our history—like Christ, Gandhi, Mother Teresa, and others, and I ask whom do we wish to model after? In whose footsteps do we wish to follow? Those of Christ, Gandhi, and Mother Teresa or in the footsteps of the person who ripped Becky O'Connell from our midst? This summer in India I read the words of a wise man: "We must continue in the face of tremendous opposition. No one is encouraging us to open, and still we must peel away the layers of the heart."

In my most enlightened moments I know that we are placed here to peel away the layers of the heart, but I do sometimes wonder what's underneath. I am often discouraged by the perception that our most basic and essential instincts include violence and survival at any cost and that it is only "common sense" to be out for Number One in a world in which dog eats dog. The spiral of hostility produced by such a mentality is best conveyed by a Somalian saying: "I and Somalia against the world. I and my clan against Somalia. I and my family against the clan. I and my brother against the family. I against my brother." Perhaps the appallingly brutal nature of the civil wars in Somalia and elsewhere in the world offers the best evidence of what happens when people adopt such a view of common sense.

In India, I heard "common sense" defined in a radically different fashion. I was staying at a health and spiritual center called Atheetha Ashram. It was an easy place to be in and commit to peeling away the layers of the heart. The physical setting was beautiful, the food was healthy, the staff was exceptionally loving, and there were inspirational tiles everywhere that carried messages such as "Life is the seed, love is the flower and laughter is the fragrance." The Swami (founder) of the ashram spoke often of the need for what he called common sense. He echoed the wisdom of David Steindl-Rast who was asked, "How can we make sense of life and of the world?" He responded, "We can make sense only to the extent to which that sense is common. The wider we stretch the sense of 'common,' the more sense we will be able to make of the world." Steindl-Rast contends that common sense tells us that below all the layers of our hearts there is a community spirit not only of people but also with animals, plants, and the whole cosmos. "What makes it so difficult to use this term is that it has been usurped by people who mean anything but common sense. They mean rather 'conventionality' and 'public opinion' which they call common sense." As I departed the ashram for much less protected environments in India and for the journey home, I vowed to conduct my own field of study as to the "true" meaning of common sense and the essential nature of humankind.

Bumping along on a forty-two-hour train ride on the way to New Delhi, I had plenty of time to contemplate and observe. I thought of hearing Anthony Padovano say that the most basic proof of our goodness is not that we're good all the time, but that we're good much more often than not. I saw the connection to Gandhi who spoke of the need to emphasize the vast majority of circumstances in which we choose not to do the evil we could have done. Gandhi did not look to the history books for evidence of our essential character. "History is only a record of every interruption of the even working force of love or of the soul." Gandhi contended that the history books do not and cannot take note of all the millions of acts of kindness and accommodation we perform each day. He asked us to watch each other rather than read the history books if we wish to discover our most essential character and soul-force. I took his advice. I watched on the crowded train as strangers shared their money, food, space, and time. The trains in India seem to stop more than they go. Each time our train stopped, a throng of vendors rushed on and down the aisles selling coffee, tea, treats to eat, and more exotic items such as stuffed cats and dogs displaying facial expressions that did little to encourage early Christmas shopping. The vendors were followed by the beggars who tried to limp, crawl, sing, weep, and moan their way into our circle of caring. Some of their maladies were so extreme that I found myself instinctively turning away and whispering to myself, "Oh my God, this is too much." But sometimes I turned back and responded or watched as someone else in some casual sacred way acknowledged our relationship with the brother or sister standing before us. I saw the kinds of actions that must have inspired the words of one of my favorite Indian sayings: "Any persons whom you have ever met, even if you have just exchanged a glance on a bus, have become part of your being and consequently you are, in some sense, responsible for them. You carry them in your heart." After more time in India and plenty more proof of the validity of Gandhi's conclusions about our essential nature, I boarded a plane to return to the U.S.A. I wondered whether I would be able to substantiate Gandhi's observations on the nonviolent character of humankind once I departed from India. I didn't have to wait very long for a chance to collect some more observations.

I don't like airports. They're much too crowded, busy, and impersonal for me. I have some of the same reactions to airports that I do to shopping malls; I feel overstimulated, unrelated, alone, and as if I want to escape as soon as possible. But on the way home from India I took note of something very revealing that happens thousands of times each day in these malls where airplanes park. In spite of the oppressive sterility of the environment, the hunger to relate cannot be ignored, and people hug like their lives depend on it. As I watched countless embraces by people getting on and off the planes, I became even more convinced that our lives do depend on love.

Within two weeks of my return from India I was in the belly of an environment that can discourage me even more than malls and airports. I was cofacilitating a nonviolence workshop for inmates in a prison in South Dakota. Many people believe that most inmates have a hole so deep inside them that they can never learn to love. By the end of our intense three days I was persuaded to the contrary. I watched as inmates hugged each other and me, wept with tears of sorrow for their families and the victims of their crimes, and spoke of the future in terms of commitment and hope. I became even more convinced of the indestructible nature of love and, behind those cold walls of prison, I glimpsed an image of love's blossom, undeterred, peaking through the layers of stone.

Now we are left with the problem of Donald Moeller, and what is underneath all the layers in his heart? I believe that below all the layers in Donald's heart, and your heart, and my heart, there is a God-seed. Meister Eckhart said: "The seed of God is in us. Given an intelligent and hard-working farmer, it will thrive and grow up with God, whose seed it is; and accordingly its fruits will be God-nature. Pear seeds grow into pear trees, nut seeds into nut trees, and God-seed into God." I believe with George Fox "that there is that of God in everyone." I suspect, however, that the thicker the membrane that we grow over our hearts, the closer to suffocation the God-seed is driven—but it never quite dies. I doubt that Donald Moeller was given much help in nourishing the God-seed within him throughout his formative years. It's not only the farmer, but also the quality of the ground that influences the progress a seed can make. One day when I was holding our three-year-old daughter Annie I spontaneously asked her, "How come you're so nice?" She clasped her hands around my neck and answered immediately—"Because you love me."

I wonder if Donald Moeller was ever asked such a question. I fear not and yet I know his God-seed lives on. Do we as a society have the capacity and the right to determine that the God-seed in Donald will never grow closer to God and that his time as one of God's farmers should end? And if we give up on Donald and execute him, what does that say about us, and how much nourishment will that act provide to the God-seed within us? I pray for Becky. I pray that we honor her memory by choosing life and the hope of redemption over death and the prospect of eternal darkness.

The Politics of Vegetables

MARIE NORD, OSF

(This isn't an article about Congressional budget negotiations or how they stood up to Bush's invasion of the Middle East. I really do want to talk about vegetables and politics—in the same breath.)

*A*bout 1972, for some unremembered reason, my political education began to escalate drastically. Maybe it was reading Gandhi's autobiography or discovering Francis Moore Lappe's *Diet for a Small Planet*. I started making connections between what I put in my mouth and what others couldn't put in theirs. I was shocked that North Americans, 6 percent of the world's population, con-

sumed about 40 percent of the world's resources. I started understanding that food is, indeed, a political issue, sometimes even a
weapon.

I decided that vegetarianism was the only responsible choice for
me. I set about trying to make my life choices reflect something a
little more fair. I decided that not eating meat could at least remind
me that others were hungry and keep me actively working for
systemic change. Plus there was the added benefit of a much health-
ier diet. (I did, however, continue to consume an occasional chicken
or fish—rationalizing that the conversion ratio for chicken, after
all, is only two pounds of grain to one pound of chicken, instead
of the twenty-one to one for beef.) For the last eighteen years,
that's where I've been. Oh, from time to time I'd think about giving
up chicken; it just seemed too complicated.

Then enters John Robbins, author of *Diet for a New America*.
I had only learned of *Diet for a New America* a few weeks before
Robbins was to speak at the University of New Mexico. I had seen
an excerpt from the book and was intrigued, so I decided to go to
his talk. I'm here to say—John Robbins is a compelling speaker.
He is gentle, accepting, affirming, and utterly convincing. He makes
you want to quit eating *all* animal products and start offering sanctuary to cows and pigs, but without inducing guilt or despair. I
came home deeply moved and determined to do better with my
choices.

His message was simple: Becoming vegetarian is the single most
radical political act you can perform today.

It's not just the facts. I think it's something about the way he
adds the facts together. For example: Every day thirty-eight thousand children die of malnutrition, and every year twenty million
people die of malnutrition. Many of us already knew that, but then
he adds: Sixty million people could be adequately nourished from
the amount of land, water, and energy freed from growing grains
and soybeans to feed U.S. livestock if North Americans reduced
their intake of meat by 10 percent! Ten percent! And you find
yourself thinking, "Gosh, anybody can do that! That's only giving
up meat about one day a week."

Then he begins to add the cost of a meat-centered diet to the
environment: The amount of U.S. topsoil lost each year to soil
erosion is four million acres, an area the size of Connecticut; 85
percent of that is "directly associated with livestock raising." The

"driving force behind the destruction of the tropical rain forests is the American meat habit." Three hundred million pounds of meat are imported annually by the U.S. from Central and South America. And one thousand species per year become extinct due to the destruction of tropical rain forests and related habitats.

Consider the reason given for U.S. military presence in the Middle East: dependence on their oil. Then consider the following: The world's petroleum reserves would last only thirteen years if all human beings ate a meat-centered diet. But, if all human beings ate vegetarian, those same reserves would last 260 years. Robbins tells us it takes seventy-eight calories of fossil fuel to get one calorie of protein from beef and only two calories of fossil fuel to get one calorie of protein from soybeans.

Just when you think there can't be more, he begins quietly talking about how livestock is raised in these United States: pig farms where animals are stacked three deep in steel cages in huge rooms; calves kept immobile and anemic to produce veal; and the routine feeding of antibiotics to livestock (55 percent of the total amount of antibiotics produced in the U.S.) resulting in many new strains of antibiotic resistant bacteria. When we degrade animals, our partners on this planet, in this way, we degrade ourselves.

The final consideration Robbins offers are the health benefits of a vegetarian lifestyle. The average meat-eating North American male runs a fifty-fifty chance of dying of a heart attack (it's a little less for women). But if that same man consumes no meat, dairy products, or eggs, his risk of dying of a heart attack is only 4 percent; if he reduces his consumption by 10 percent, it is 9 percent. Women who eat meat daily have an almost four times greater chance of getting breast cancer, when compared to women who eat meat less than once a week. The average measurable bone loss of female meat-eaters at age sixty-five is 35 percent, while for vegetarians it is only 18 percent.

Consider: There were originally twelve official "basic Food groups" before the meat, dairy, and egg industries applied enormous political pressure on behalf of their products. Now there are four, and two of the four are animal products. The National Dairy Council, it turns out, is the main source for nutritional education materials found in our schools. Our children (and all the rest of us as well) are brainwashed with the slogans of the National Dairy Council. Milk is advertised as nature's most perfect food. Well, it is—for calves, who have four stomachs, will double their weight in forty-seven days, and weigh about one thousand pounds in a year. But for humans: "20 percent of Caucasians and up to 90 percent of Black and Asian people have no lactase in their intestines," so they can't digest milk. Looks like it might be time to take back the task of nutritional education from the National Dairy Council.

"By 1980, consumption of grains and potatoes fell to half their 1900 levels, while the amount of fats in the American diet more than doubled. Such drastic dietary changes cannot occur without very significant consequences—not only in the public health, but in the economy and the environment as well . . . "

I feel that this is an area where we still have control. We can decide what we eat. Robbins' father and uncle are the founders of the Baskin-Robbins ice cream empire. Robbins claims that he had an ice cream cone-shaped swimming pool when he was a kid. He changed his lifestyle . . . Radically, Grace . . . So, don't be afraid. Start from where you are and go for it. What have you got to lose? Just heart disease, osteoporosis, strokes, kidney stones, a dozen different kinds of cancer, hypertension, diverticulosis, hemorrhoids, obesity, asthma, etc., etc., etc. VIVA TOFU!!!

All the facts used in this article were taken from an excerpt from John Robbins, Diet for a New America, *called "Realities." This piece and information about Earth Save, a nonprofit, environmental educational organization founded by Robbins and his wife, are available from: Earth Save, 706 Frederick Street, Santa Cruz, CA 95062-2205.*

How Do We Help?

RICHARD ROHR, OFM

Nothing feels better than helping and being helped—especially when the problem is immediate and there is a need for resolution. One is able to feel good about oneself for being generous, while the other feels the relief that comes from knowing that one is not alone in the universe. Helping feels "Christian" on both sides, so much so that most people assume that's what it's all about. You are good and religious if you help other people, and we all have a right to expect God-fearing people to help us. I know it sounds right, but I don't believe it anymore. In fact, I think do-goodism often keeps us from the true help that the human soul is waiting for. Jesus refuses to resort too quickly or finally to social action, until he knows that more fundamental longings are also being addressed: the desire for soul, the need for meaning and communion, the hunger for the Other. "Humankind does not live on bread alone, but on every word that comes from the mouth of God" (Matt. 4:4).

After twenty years of counseling, pastoring, and clumsy attempts at helping other people, I am coming to a not so obvious but compelling conclusion: Much of our helping is like hoping for first-class accommodations on the Titanic. It feels good at the moment but it is going nowhere. The big tear in the hulk is not addressed, and we are surprised when people drown, complain, or resort to lifeboats. Most of the people I have tried to fix still need fixing. The situation changed but the core was never touched.

But what is the core? And how do we touch it? What does it mean essentially to *help* another person? If we can find the answer to these questions, we are coming close to what the world religions mean by true ministry. It is absolutely unlike any other form of helping. It has many counterfeits and disguises. What Jesus, Buddha, Confucius, the saints, and the prophets are talking about is the *Absolute Help,* which alone is worthy of the name—the radical help that none of us can give to another. We can only point to it and promise that it is there. That is the first and final work of all true religion. All else is secondary.

Call it grace, enlightenment, peak experience, baptism in the Spirit, revelation, consciousness, growth, or surrender, but until such a threshold is passed, people are never helped in any true, lasting sense. After the early stages of identity and belonging are worked through, real transformation does not seem to take place apart from some kind of contact with the Transcendent or Absolute. We now live in a secular culture that is largely afraid to talk about such contact except in either fundamentalist or vague New Age language. Neither is sufficient to name the depth or the personal demand of the true God encounter. What characterizes the trustworthy conversion experience is a profound sense of meeting *Another,* who names me personally and yet calls me to a task beyond myself. Therapeutic healing will always be an effect, but it is never the goal itself or even a concern. One's own wholeness pales into insignificance in relationship to the Wholeness one is now delighting in.

Too much fixing and problem-solving are often an avoidance of that very "breakdown," that collapse into Mercy which alone will finally help us. The philosophy and spirituality of the twelve-step programs warn us against any well-meaning codependency that merely maintains the good feeling of helping and being helped. Wholistic healers will help us to realize that we will need help and that their job is to help us break down creatively and in a safe container so that we can seek the Real Help. Certainly that has been the therapy of the traditional shaman, Zen master, or spiritual guide.

True ministry does not give answers and take away pain too quickly, but, in fact, leads one deeper into mystery and then gives the courage and surety to remain there—"like a child in its mother's arms, as content as an infant that has been weaned" (Ps. 131:2). Such ministry is not widely appreciated in a culture of instant gratification and fix-it shops. There are few teachers of patience, listening, and observation who would instruct us as Joseph Campbell does: "Where we had thought to find an abomination, we will find a god; where we had thought to slay another, we shall slay ourselves; where we had thought to travel outward, we shall come to the center of our own existence; and where we had thought to be alone, we shall be with all the world." Passing through these gates of mystery, we enter into the temple where we are healed almost in spite of ourselves.

This salvation (*salus*-healing) is not dependent on feeling or any person's response to me. It is not a theory believed, a theology proclaimed, or a group that gives one identity. It is an inner clarity that forever allows one to recognize bogus authority and pseudo-surrender. This salvation cannot be acquired by a simple process of self-examination, new insight, or ego-possession. It is a gift *received* when the will has given up control and we are standing in that threshold place which allows us to see anew. What we see are sacred signs, and the true helper will encourage me to get out of the way so I can see them. Suffering, failure, rejection, and loss can lead to this same threshold. Grace then walks us into the temple. Sacred signs in the form of stories, images, symbols, or dreams are usually not rational but a breakdown of logic that serves as a character armor for the soul. For example, the strong man finds himself completely disarmed in the presence of a little baby—through which he meets God.

This experience of divine breakthrough can be had by people who are still very neurotic by clinical standards. Holiness is not necessarily wholeness. Sometimes the preoccupation and expectation of human wholeness actually keep us from the deeper longing and thirsting for justice that is probably the real thing. Often the best we can do is recognize our neurosis. The help that is offered is just enough to keep us from destroying ourselves and making life impossible for those around us. But our neuroses do not go away.

Victory over sin is never total but rather a victory over sin's power to overwhelm us or defeat us. The sacred signs allow us to live with and walk with and through our sin to God. God's help does not readjust our false self or polish up our self-image. Instead, God shows us the depths of our emptiness and sin so that we have nothing more to shock or humiliate us.

History will judge this age for at least two heresies: an educated secularism which has good answers but is incapable of teaching spiritual journey and surrender, and an almost total identification of salvation with merely psychic or therapeutic experience.

The truth that we must live is to be ready and awake so that we might see the sacred signs. If we are free from ourselves, we will be free for God. If we are open to true help, capable of awe and desire, we will be found by an awful and awesome lover.

The Gifts of Andrew

JUSTINE BUISSON

Already the gifts of Hurricane Andrew are drifting out of sight in my part of Dade County. We are back in the old place, almost. Yet we can never really go back to those complacent streets, that layer of green between earth and sky that hid our neighbors' houses, that sense of security behind closed doors.

Gifts, you ask? Yes. For three weeks we became powerless—no electricity (or water for those with wells), disrupted food supply and mail service, debris-filled roads, destruction of our lush environment. A few days after the storm a neighbor and I went reconnoitering for batteries and cans of Sterno. Empty-handed, we drove down the highway and saw a crowd outside Publix supermarket. We joined other scavengers there rummaging through shopping carts among defrosted boxes of waffles and microwave meals. I looked at the faces of these fellow survivors, dazed and yet connected in a new way, and I thought, "We are one of Them now, the dispossessed."

Yes, my family and neighbors and I had been set down in a strange land. But there were gifts in exchange for losses. We learned to live by the sun. We were drawn outside our houses—to the sunlight, the sound of birds miraculously still alive, to cool little breezes coming through the heat, to the presence of one another and a new sharing, as well as a sense of survivor guilt at having been spared the real misery further south.

Miami isn't traditionally a friendly place. Too many transients, refugees, get-rich-quickers, and drug dealers have marked its inhabitants with wariness. Andrew changed this overnight. We were all needy, we recognized each other, we dropped our guard. My Cuban neighbors who have city water pulled a hose into my yard so I could fill a pail for essential washing. A family of Jehovah Witnesses across the street invited me for dinner cooked on their camp stove. We all shared bottles of water, bags of ice, food, and batteries. Forced outside to find sunlight and a breeze, we chatted with each other, got to know a few things we didn't know. I was the only one of my block with a working phone, so there were visits to my kitchen all day long.

And day was short. Every afternoon my children and grandchildren came for a swim and a cookout, but by 7:30 it was getting dark. My son lit the Coleman lantern for me and they said goodbye. I sat on the patio receiving the breeze and watching the last Army helicopters heading back from Homestead and Florida City. By eight the darkness and ensuing silence had closed in. I tried to read by lantern light, but the heat it emitted drove me to the pool for a final dip. The water there, for all the silt and leaves at the bottom, became holy for me. Stepping down into the cool wetness held a mysterious healing. Under the waxing moon I felt closer to nature than ever before.

That connection had begun in the early morning hours of the hurricane. Three adults, two children, two dogs, and four cats, we huddled in a small bedroom of my children's house, listening. The shutters rattled like lawn chairs, the walls vibrated and sweated, our ears popped as the pressure dropped. Surreal yelping sounds issued from the other side of the house. The experience was so powerful that it left no room for thought. Nature is a life-giver and a nurturer, but she is also a destroyer like the Hindu Kali. That dark force was at work here. We were reduced to feeling— fear, awe. I tried to tell myself we were in God's hands. This power was God's, and we were in the midst of it. There was no escape.

The next morning we sat in the kitchen silenced by the devastation becoming visible. All the trees were down, either snapped in two or uprooted; electric lines swung and looped across yards. Their carport was gone, and the roof over a bedroom. We walked down the street with others, stepping over branches and shingles, past houses with every window blown in, roofs clawed away. My son drove me home, sixty blocks north, down an unrecognizable highway into a neighborhood with no landmarks left. We didn't know then that the eye of the hurricane had passed over Homestead and Florida City to the south. My house was hidden behind fallen trees, but was otherwise undamaged except for some torn screens. But, of course, no one had electricity or water that first week.

Later that day, sitting dazed on my own patio, in view of fallen trees and branches sheared of leaves, I felt the connection of the night before, but a kinder one. A family of parrots jumped and scolded on one remaining bare branch above me. They sounded just like neighbors. "Did you hear? Did you see?" I became part of the outdoors, feeling a breeze the air conditioner doesn't allow, hearing birds and neighbors' conversations, with a clearer view of houses than before. As time passed, the sound of helicopters and chain saws would drown out other sounds. But the feeling of connectedness remained.

The first Sunday Mass at my church was stripped of superfluity. We sat on folding chairs in the Family Center, advised to stay in our seats because of the heat. Our pastor wore only a stole around his shoulders over a short-sleeved shirt. As we sang, "The Lord hears the cry of the poor," I realized that *we* are the Lord. How else would his work be done in the world? So I volunteered to help distribute food and clothing there.

In my neighborhood we began to depend on one another, on little gifts of kindness. And on the light of the sun. As he was dying, the poet Goethe asked for "more light." Did he need more, or see more? The meaning of his words will forever be a mystery.

For me now since the hurricane, light itself is a mystery. I had forgotten that before this century there was only gaslight, and before that kerosene and oil. The chandeliers of Versailles were lit with hundreds of candles, and aristocrats lit candles to find their way to bed.

When my power was restored three weeks after Andrew struck, at first I forgot to turn on the light and worked in the daylight that came into my house. Turning on the faucet and seeing water spurt out was miraculous. I began to wonder about reality. Was real life what I had just left behind, when I was powerless like people in the Third World? Or is reality life inside an airtight house cooled and fueled by electricity, insulated from sounds outside—the little breezes that play with the trees, and neighbors' voices, neighbors' needs?

Now I can think again, as I couldn't during the time of heat and sweat. I can think about meanings. There was an interconnection I experienced as never before. And a deep awe of the mystery of which we are all a part, pretend though we may to be apart from it. I think I can see more clearly the difference between artificial and natural comforts, between what is impermanent and what endures. There are children in Dade County who will never trust the permanence of walls again. Will they learn to depend on something more substantial? Or will their disorientation last a lifetime? And the old people who never had much and now have nothing, what will they trust? The kindness of strangers? Migrant families are still sitting in little tents, sweltering in the heat, wading through mud when it rains. For how long will they continue to be so needy, so abject? For the first time in their lives many South Floridians experienced human misery firsthand. They became the Anawim they had seen on TV screens in countries to the south, or they ministered to them.

All these questions are gifts of Andrew, if only we can interiorize them, learn from them, use them to cut through the invisible walls we live behind, pretending to be secure. Then Andrew-Kali can be not only the Destroyer, but the restorer of proportion, our gate into the real world.

Church and Sexuality: Naming the Shadow

CHRISTINA SPAHN

*L*ately I've thought often of a priest I met early in my six years as religious education director for the Archdiocese of Santa Fe. In order to get a sense of who and what was where, I had decided to visit every parish in the diocese, meet parish staffs, and personally deliver the new religious education directories. My reception at the second parish was far from hospitable, and I was discouraged. Was this really the way to get acquainted? With some dread, I approached the third church office, in northeastern New Mexico. It was almost noon, so when the elderly pastor opened the door, I thrust the directory into his hands, introduced myself, and told him that I was sure he was getting ready to eat and that I was leaving. He looked quizzical at this behavior and invited me out for lunch—a most healing gesture!

Some time later I happened to be facilitating a catechists' workshop in his parish when this same priest interrupted to announce that a much loved organist had just died. Tears coursed down his cheeks as he described this woman's goodness and commitment, and I remember being touched bv the love and vulnerability of this gentle old man.

A few months after nis retirement, he was convicted of ordering pornography through the mail.

For the last several months, the Albuquerque media has been full of tales of clerical pedophilia and illicit sexual liaisons. Five priests and our Archbishop have been indicted or accused. The situation is not unique to New Mexico, and a question the church must face is: Why?

The most immediate response, rapidly advocated and accompanied with promises of counseling, out-of-court cash settlements, and "anything else we can do" for the victims, is that "Father has a problem." Largely because of public outrage, church officials have been challenged to greater sensitivity toward victims. But too often, even today, the priest is scurried away and as much distance as possible is placed between him and the church he once served—as if the two were not connected.

This is not meant to excuse the crimes committed by clergy who have violated both public and private trust (and vulnerable children). However, to focus only on them is to be concerned with the symptoms rather than the disease. It is to deny systemic evil in the church and society which cannot be disguised or avoided simply by punishing the perpetrators.

From at least the time of Augustine, who decried the out-of-rational-control nature of passion, questioned the morality of intercourse except for the procreation of children, and taught the inferiority of women, the church has delivered a mixed message regarding sexuality: Conjugal love is good but virginity is better (in the Middle Ages, monks and nuns were known as "spiritualists" while the rest of humanity was labeled "carnalists"); the body, as well as all material creation, is suspect; using rhythm for birth control is permissible but using the pill is not, and so on. The official line has been positive in its assessment of sexuality and the holiness of marriage, but underlying that has been a pervasive negativity revealed in both ritual (only in recent times has the rite of matrimony been moved into the church sanctuary) and regulation (a married permanent deacon is still prohibited from remarrying upon the death of his wife). Neither of these examples is an endorsement for marriage as a vocation to holiness!

Because the church has so long denied its feminine face, its treatment of sexuality has focused on principles, analysis, and rules. It has largely neglected the nonrational, emotive components of the human soul which have gone underground and become subversive. What I think we are seeing in the present crisis is a personal and communal shadow (that part of oneself that is unknown, unwanted, and denied) surfacing with an aberrant twist here and there in the criminal and sad behavior of men such as the elderly priest.

Celibacy is the way to holiness for some people. However, in a church that has not come to terms with sexuality or embraced both its giftedness and its challenges, is it not possible that celibacy offers an escape, and the hierarchical structure provides a cover?

What I believe we are experiencing now is the cumulative effect of centuries of a head-in-the-sand mentality that has relied on power, peer pressure, and self-image to keep people in line. Maybe in another age, when priests were unquestioned parish authorities, this approach "worked." However, with the priestly role unraveling and many priests searching for a sense of identity and purpose, some are becoming sexually involved in ways that reveal not only their own problems but also those of the system they represent.

A friend of mine makes the point that just as marriage is learned, so, too, is celibacy. One needs to work at an integration through which this choice is life-giving and part of the unique holiness to which one is called. However, since celibacy is a requirement for ordination, a discipline imposed on all aspiring to the Roman Catholic priesthood, in some cases it is not chosen. Without this element of conscious choice, some priests have not engaged in the necessary reconciliation of the need for intimacy with their life commitment—a struggle that is imperative for the growth and healthy development of every person, married or single.

When one's sexuality is not integrated, this powerful and primal force moves into the unconscious where it is still active but cut off from conscious discernment and choice. Dwelling in the shadow, sexuality exerts tremendous influence and can find expression in a wide variety of compensatory and explicitly sexual behavior—in a way that is neither acknowledged nor "owned." This results in a fragmented person who is unaware of motivations impelling personal behavior.

For centuries, the church has not dealt adequately with sexuality or its own masculine/feminine identity. In this failure, we have amassed an increasingly looming shadow that cries for recognition and integration.

The stories of the victims are tragic; those of the priests are sad. The church can respond through disaster control and simply deal with litigation. Or we can recognize this as a moment of grace, admit our historic role in the crisis, and respond to the clarion call to repentance, conversion, and healing.

Letter from Richard

RICHARD ROHR, OFM

*D*ear Friends,

Sometimes the voices of self-doubt assault me: Maybe I am too hard on the U.S. Maybe I have just moved to the political left and it is not really Gospel that guides me. Maybe pragmatic problem-solving *is* really the best way. Maybe our political leaders are basically sincere and honest men. And on and on.

Then this war is provoked and concocted and I realize: It's even worse than I thought! There is no truth at work here, only disguised and denied self-interest. Like Isaiah I want to say, "O my people, your rulers mislead you and destroy the road you walk on . . . . By what right do they crush my people and grind the faces of the poor?" (Isa. 3:12, 15). And I know the accusation applies to both Saddam Hussein and George Bush. The one's poorly educated and terrorized people follow him to death, and the other's college educated and supposedly free people do the same. Somehow the second is harder to comprehend, especially when you are accused of being unpatriotic if you don't buy the lie. Apparently we are just supposed to be thinking and free people until the first shot is fired. Then we must all go into a coma state and wave flags. At the same time, I know that deep and unconscious images are at work in the American and Iraqi souls. Logic, truth, and consistency have little sway here, and we are dealing with archetypes that capture the very core of persons and groups.

First, I am convinced that blood is male milk. It is men's way of nurturing and protecting. It touches something both primal and romantic and so urgent that otherwise thinking people are paralyzed before it. When blood is threatened, spilled, or wasted, all the images of family, loyalty, love, and literature come into play. And as Shakespeare said, "Conscience would make cowards of us all."

Men especially are attracted to warrior energy. All the hunters, gatherers, defenders, knights, samurais, and swordsmen are, in fact, telling us something good about focus, determination, and courage for the common good. As men have lost their clear goal of a larger good beyond themselves, it has largely been taken up by women for purposes of children, relationship, and issues of justice. Women need to help men keep their focus and determination for broader purposes than private prestige and power. How said that men march off to give blood for lies, and women cheer them on. Both seem in the grip of an archetype that will destroy them.

The perennial weakness of warrior energy, according to Robert Moore, is that it lacks breadth and depth. Focus and determination are good, but that's not everything. The secret of a good warrior is that one must be in tutelage to a good leader. The warrior without a good "king" or "queen" has no wisdom, no temperance, no balance, no final goals beyond tracking, fighting, killing the enemy. Witness the domestic policy of Bush and Hussein, and witness the aimless lives of far too many old soldiers who never die but just fade away. We are led by men who are warriors of a small sort but surely not wise kings. They have no vision beyond winning, and they are foolishly leading another generation of men who seem to have no vision beyond following.

The warrior archetype is not going away. Our job is to educate and redefine the warrior in the way that Moses, David, Jesus, Mary Magdalene, and Dorothy Day lived out their passion. Warrior energy is not in its essence wrong. It takes warrior energy to see through and stand against mass illusions of our time and be willing to pay the price of disobedience. It takes warrior energy to see through the soft rhetoric of "support our troops" which cleverly diverts us from the objective evil of this war. It takes warrior energy to march to a different drum, disbelieve the patriotic trivia, and rebelieve in the tradition of nonviolence, civil resistance, and martyrdom. Young men and women who take oaths of secular governments are not martyrs in any classic sense; rather, they are soldiers offering to kill for Caesar. We Christians were taught a very different way—the way of the cross.

The U.S. instinctively knows that real warrior energy has been sublimated into activities of business and sports. We are desperately searching for something heroic, transcendent, or self-sacrificing. The recent "support our troops" rallies have the fervor of worship services; the tearful songs and sweet sentiment seem like ritual romance, with yellow ribbons secular substitutes for prayers and fasting. While not doubting the sincerity of most participants, it's still amazing that Christians buy this shallow pseudo-spirituality.

The answer is very old-fashioned and one that you might expect from me. My Father, Francis of Assisi, said it simply and well: "I am the Herald of the Great King." Francis never stopped being a warrior-knight. He just found a greater king. His image of self and victory changed. His goals grew broader, his heart deeper. He was still ready to spill blood for the cause, but now it led him to a personal visit to the Sultan in Egypt in the very midst of the bloody Christian Crusades. He was prepared to offer his male milk, his blood, not for the violent death of any enemy but for the nonviolent victory of love.

Warrior energy needs to be wholly dedicated and given *somewhere* or to *something,* whether the *somewhere* or *something* is worthy or true. It must be focused and released for the warrior to know that she or he is alive and has character. Both in Iraq and in America the goals are actually unimportant; it's just important that the warriors stand for something or someone. Our work is to find worthy causes and goals to receive worthy warrior energy.

I do not know if the majority of people will be ready for such a path. In the light of the past months' events, it would appear that very few are on a path of integrity. (One day before the fighting, almost eighty percent opposed the war; one day after almost eighty percent supported it!)

But our job is to continue to proclaim a path and to make it possible. That is the work of the Center for Action and Contemplation. I am grateful for the many who walk with us and show us the way.

Peace and every good,
Richard Rohr, OFM

Part II

TO LOVE
TENDERLY

The Call to Emptiness

AVIS CROWE

*I*n my late thirties I went in to the wilderness of my soul. It was a long journey into the heart of paradox, for I discovered that in the emptiness of my life was the ground of fulfillment. All of this happened at Pendle Hill, a Quaker center for study and contemplation near Phladelphia. It is as far removed from a true wilderness as one can find. An alternative adult living-learning community, it is also an arboretum with lush grounds abounding with trees, flowers, space—and people who are all on a spiritual quest.

I had already gone back to school once, the "real" kind, some years earlier. I had left New York City and the world of commercial television production, in search of . . . what? Something that would fill the void, satisfy the inchoate longing that had dogged me for years yet remained unmet in spite of career changes, lifestyle experimentation, a dozen addresses, and even more personal entanglements. A graduate degree provided temporary satisfaction. I had recognized the need for drastic change and had acted on it; I felt a sense of accomplishment and had a paper in hand that proved I was capable. Confirmation came when I landed a satisfying job as an art administrator. I had even found love and looked forward to marriage. I gave up my job and moved halfway across the country. Then the first domino fell—the love affair ended and the rest of my life came tumbling down around me. I was nothing at all; I was unlovable, unemployed, and alone. I felt very empty. Like a wounded animal I limped back to the East Coast, crawled into the dark hole of depression, and stayed there for nearly two years.

As I looked back much later, I could see that the amazing grace of the song had been my constant companion during that period. It took the form of caring friends who insisted I get help; it led me to a Quaker meeting where I recognized the spiritual nature of my longing. It was grace that helped me find a skilled therapist who received my tears, helped me through the tangled byways of the past, and set me on a path of healing. It was grace that drew me to Koinonia Partners in Georgia, where I began to learn firsthand about community and radical church and where the true spiritual journey began. And it was grace that led me to Pendle Hill, with its peculiar curriculum of classes that included such titles as *Compassion and Community, Monasticism,* and *The Plain People.* A class called *The Wilderness Journey,* taught by Sonnie Cronk, was pivotal for me. More than pivotal, it was transforming.

During the ten weeks of the class I walked with the likes of The Desert Fathers, Thomas Merton, Caryll Houselander, The Little Sisters of Jesus, and many others. In their company I experienced the interior desert and found amazing possibilities there. The desert, I discovered, was not a wasteland at all but a unique terrain that is home to a wide variety of living things. I looked inside myself, and where before I had seen nothing, I found a woman waiting to be born. I had come face-to-face with paradox and felt at home there.

Midway through the course, we went on a silent weekend retreat at an historic Quaker Meeting House in rural Pennsylvania Dutch country. We had been encouraged to think about our own emptiness. In the silence I stared into the fire, wrote in my journal and watched out the window as Amish horse-drawn buggies passed by in the winter chill. Some of the words I reflected on were those of St. John of the Cross:

> A sail can catch the wind and be used to manoeuver a boat only because it is so frail. It is the weakness of the sail that makes it sensitive to the wind.

It was a new concept for me, but I knew it as Truth, knew it physically, in the center of my body. For the first time I began to have an inkling that in my loneliness, the place where I felt most empty, was strength. But it was just an inkling. The word *empty* was laden with negative experience and assumptions for me. To be empty was to be hungry, needy, unloved, and unacceptable—a condition to be remedied with food, career, husband, and children. All of these eluded me except food, which was both comfort and curse. Yet here were John of the Cross, and others, knocking that askew and pointing to an extraordinary notion: that exmptiness, that weakness, was where the real strengh lay! That a vessel must be empty in order to be filled; that to be a channel, one must be free of inpediments; that the reed flute must be hollow in order to receive the player's breath; that to be empty is the way, in fact, to becoming full.

In a moment of revelation I realized that emptiness is NOT nothingness, which had been my greatest fear. Rather, it is the foundation of a truly vibrant faith and action. I felt almost breathless as these ideas first crept, than tumbled, into my consciousness, into my bloodstream. I heard in them an invitation, a call to stand in the midst of my own emptiness and live there for a while, experience it fully, claim it—even *pro*claim it. If I could do this, I just might come to a point of receptivity at which transformation could truly happen.

I wrote in my journal:

> I've turned the corner. My perception has shifted: from aloneness as something to regret and grieve over, to something positive, something to be celebrated as the condition that has been given me. What I have NOT been given is as much a gift as are the things I have been given (which I am also beginning to see and acknowledge!). I feel ripe and open and available, as though the ideas and words I've been reading and struggling with are being made of flesh . . . mine.

But that was in 1982. The sharpness of insight and discovery has faded over time and in the wake of the extraordinary turns my life has taken, I had gone to Pendle Hill as a student for a year and had seen the glass of my life half empty. During four more years on the staff it became half full and then overflowed. In those five years I began to see things from the perspective of the downside-up kingdom, as Sonnie Cronk liked to characterize the Kingdom of God. In the process of embracing my own emptiness I opened myself to possiblity for the first time. Gifts beyond any earlier imaginings were given to me as a result: a life-companion, time in South Africa, ministries that opened up at Pendle Hill teaching courses in Journal Writing and leading retreats, work I was able to continue during our Cape Town sojourn. And now, after years of living in apartments or other people's houses, I have my first home here in New Mexico. It has been a decade of unexpected blessings; a time of filling up with life's abundance.

But as this winter approached, I could feel the tide turning. In nature there is a cycle of seasons. The fruitfulness of spring and summer give way to autumnal shedding of leaves that reveal starkly beautiful skeletons of trees, and then to the lengthening darkness and the hard ground of winter. Fields lie fallow. Bulbs are planted and wait for spring, unseen beneath the crusty earth. This cycle repeats itself over and over, each one a time of recovery and of preparation. There is in me a similar cycle. My life has become so full that there is not much room for the working of the spirit. I have all but abandoned the regular journal writing and periodic retreats that had become essential parts of my life. I find myself moving too fast, talking too much, becoming short-tempered and resentful of people. Almost without realizing it I have allowed myself to get caught up in activity and now find myself living in the shallows, no longer anchored in the deep.

Once I had chosen Emptiness as the theme for the retreat I will lead at the Center in February, I realized with a start that it was *I* who was being called to emptiness. It was I who was being reminded that it is time once again to lie fallow, to sink into's winter's embrace, to let the leaves fall away; the leaves of activity and personal plans, needs, dreams, as well as the recurring hunger for approval. When my husband accepted an invitation to go to England, I decided to remain here. I think now that I was acting on an inner knowledge that I needed to slow down and empty out. Perhaps grace is at it again! I fight emptiness, know how hard it is to go into the wilderness. But I know, too, that God comes with me into that place, leads me through it to the other side where I am able to live more authentically and closer to the roots of my faith. In emptying out I can once again become a hollow reed, to be played by the One who has created all things.

The Cross of Jesus and Human Suffering

RICHARD ROHR, OFM

The language of the cross may be illogical to those who are not on the way to salvation, but those of us who are on the way see it as God's power to save.

Cor. 1:18

When Christianity loses the doctrine and power of the cross as its central strategy, it becomes a false and impotent religion. When this happens, as it has again and again, the Lord renews his people by calling them back—usually in spite of themselves—to the "way of the cross."

This is happening dramatically in our time in the churches of the poor and persecuted, particularly those of Central and South America. Their lives and deaths appear to be a crisis and grace for the churches of North America and Europe. Through their faith and forgiveness, Jesus is calling all of his church back to the doctrine and power of his cross, "to tell us what God has guaranteed, the only knowledge of him as the crucified Christ," (Cor. 2:2).

Most of Christian history has seen the cross as a password, a sacred omen, a bit of magic that changed the agenda, something to be grateful for—supremely so—and therefore to be worshipped and used as the symbol of our faith. And rightly so, yet with a terribly shallow and evasive understanding. The cross became something we could feel sorry, pious, or religious about, or grateful for, but it seldom named a way of life that we would choose and actively serve. The false doctrine of the cross became the "substitutionary" worship of Jesus instead of the call and strategy of Jesus.

The cross is precisely that difficulty, privation, persecution, and misunderstanding that comes into one's life when one attempts to live the Reign of God in this world—not just the sufferings and hardships. The cross, as in Jesus' life, is freely and consciously "allowed" as the necessary price to break through the world's lies and false promises.

The cross is our obedience to the price of truth and love—with no assurance that it is going to work. As in the life of Jesus, the cross leads us to perfect faith. Love led to its logical conclusion demands that we trust in a Goodness and a Life beyond our own. The doctrine of the cross says that no lie can live forever, but there is a price to the breaking down of the lie. It is Love become active and personally engaged. Finally, there is no other word for love except sacrifice, the cross, "laying down one's life for one's friends" (John 15:13). The cross is *doing the truth*.

While the affluent and unpersecuted churches of the North have abandoned the life of the cross and pursued happiness or survival in this world, the Christians of the South have been led to a different kind of joy and survival based on the cross of Jesus. Thus their lives have the power to shake, subvert, save, and sanctify our churches—precisely through and because of the cross! We are forced to recognize that we are "only strangers and nomads on this earth" (Heb. 11:13) when some like ourselves are free to scorn the rewards and comforts of this world in favor of a greater vision—the coming of the Reign of God.

Yes, the cross is our salvation. It makes us holy. It frees us and liberates us for God and the Great Picture. It "opens the gates of heaven" by closing off our loyalties to hell. It "buys" us the truth which is always expensive in this world. Through the cross Jesus "paid the price" not so that we would not have to, but so that we would in fact know that there is a price for truth and love and it is *everything*.

Holiness has always been a very difficult concept to describe or define. People usually settle for an image of sweetness, soft piety, churchiness, humility, or asceticism. But I believe holiness can only be recognized by its effect in others. No one can claim it for himself or herself, as if it were a possession. Holiness is just that quality in a person which calls others to healing, forgiveness, conversion, and liberation from the self.

The Christians of Central America, the cross of Jesus, are *threatening us* with holiness! Now we have really to admit how much we want to be holy, how much we want to be like Jesus, how much we love God's Reign.

A Life Centered
on the Breath

MARY VINEYARD

*B*etween May 31 and June 5 Ruben and Maria Habito came to Albuquerque to lead twenty of us in a retreat that combined copius amounts of Zen sitting with teaching on the spiritual Exercises of St. Ignatius. Trained and practiced in both Christianity and Buddhism, in Ignatian spirituality and Zen, having lived and studied in Germany, the Philippines, China, and Japan, these two lovely teachers were uniquely suited to guide our group, which varied widely in age, nationality, life issues, religious perspective, and familiarity with Ignatius and Zen. With great understanding and openness they listened to our questions and needs; with great clarity they offered us information and insight; and with great calm they modeled the qualities of the spiritual life we long to live.

In Japan a Zen retreat is called a Sesshin, which means "an encounter of the heart." Our intent for these five days was to make ourselves available, to dispose ourselves for such an encounter. We were to listen, to still our bodies, quiet our hearts, empty our minds so that it might become possible for us to be met, spoken to, and touched.

The structure by which we were to create this openness consisted of maintaining silence throughout the retreat, Zen sitting for about six hours per day, and daily teachings and private interviews with Ruben.

Zen is a Japanese translation of a Chinese word, *ch'an*, the two characters of which mean, roughly, "divine" and "simple." So Zen is simple and at the same time very difficult, just as the divine is everywhere always present, yet often very hard to discern or become aware of. We sit, very still, facing a wall, spine straight, eyes half closed, following our breath, listening, listening. "Making our whole being something that listens." and what we listen for is everything, the everything that we are totally connected to. We listen so that we can become perfectly aware of the mystery; so that we can live in total freedom; so that we can experience complete gratitude. And so we can hear the cries of the world.

It is one of the beautiful paradoxes of Zen that one faces a wall, looks away from the world—both in its beauty and in its sorrow—so that one can love and understand it better. But this paradox is evidence of its trustworthiness, for a mark of any true and deeply good spiritual practice would be its ability to lead us always back into communion with all beings. Referring to the Central American custom of honoring the dead with the expression "Presente!", Ruben encouraged us to allow the suffering of the world to remain present in us, to pray the psalm of the crucified world: "My God, my God, why have you forsaken me?" He suggested that an appropriate way to meditate on the passion of Christ, as the Ignatian Exercises require, is to pay attention to the ways in which the earth is now being crucified. On the wall of our meditation room hung a map entitled "Endangered Earth," on which we could visualize the suffering of our planet, its plants and animals, and its human inhabitants. Ruben reminded us that it is always those who live closest to the earth who suffer first and most when the earth is threatened.

The danger, though, in allowing ourselves to hear the cries of so many suffering beings, and our own cries as well, is that we might become overwhelmed by them, might despair of ever being able to do enough to help. Ruben's answer to this temptation is shockingly simple, "divinely simple." We are only doing enough when we are giving our all in every breath. When we realize that everything is given with each breath and we choose, in return, with each breath, to return everything we have, then we are doing enough. And it is easy enough to know, in any moment, whether we are in fact perfectly aware of the mystery, wholly open, completely grateful, truly listening. And it is possible to live in such a stance, for one moment at a time. False guilt can evaporate and real responsiveness can appear.

Indeed, this momentary, breath-based way of being is Ruben's description of a spiritual life: a life in or of the Spirit; a life centered on the breath, paying attention, being aware, listening, receiving, giving, breathing in and breathing out, acknowledging the bipolar interpenetrating essential nature of life; breathing breaths shared by the whole planet—dolphins and kapok trees—Salvadorans and Iraqis.

And so, with this instruction, we practiced. Sitting, facing our own piece of wall. Six hours each day, nailing ourselves to our cushions, breathing through our pains, our fatigue, our doubts and distractions. Ruben told us, "Don't just do something. Sit there." Sit there and wait. Sit there and listen. Sit there and breathe. Don't think. Thinking is less, much less, than being. Sit there and watch what happens. Watch the demons rise, the thousand and one thoughts and feelings, memories, fears, imaginings, all the wild inhabitants of the mind.

And as the hours and day flowed or sometimes trudged past, each of us found something unique happening within us. We learned how much the mind can chatter, how long it takes for it to become quiet. How rare silence and stillness are, and how precious. How deep compassion is, how much we are tied to all beings. How understanding and encounter often come just beyond the edge of endurance. How closely we can bond to those with whom we sit in silence.

And I believe that, as we parted, it is fair to say that we had all been met. Somewhere in at least one of those moments, one of those breaths, we had encountered the One we were seeking, the very source of compassion and understanding, the One who is everywhere and in us all, the One whose very breath we are.

Journey to the Center

LINDA HARDY

I had stopped by the Center to use the chapel one morning when I happened to look out the back window and see that there was too much summer out there for me to ignore—too much green, too much light, too many leafy shadows flung like nets in my direction. I was held fast by this image of the beauty and bounty and promise of summer, and by the knowledge that this might be my last summer here.

My husband, Dan, is in the process of applying for fellowships, so next July we may be starting a year somewhere else. Where we settle permanently depends on where he gets a job after that.

I don't mean to imply that I've had no say in the matter. Up until a few months ago, in fact, I was so opposed to moving that he was getting used to the idea of taking his last year of training here, although that wasn't his preference. But one day when the subject came up I realized, "Yes, I can do that." It didn't feel like giving in (I would never do that on anything so important) or like sacrificing my interest to his (that would have made me feel immediately resentful). It had the completely novel feel of, if not letting go, at least loosening my grip a little. I was willing to go some places, but not others.

When I was single, the most important life decisions were always the easiest ones for me to make, because in something that crucial, all I had to do was consult my own heart. My own inner voice was strong enough to drown out all other considerations. Now, with two children, there's a lot more clamoring of voices and a lot more muddling through. Even when I can hear my own voice, I can't often act on it.

But in this decision, I heard a new voice. It was still coming from my own heart, but this time it was saying, "You don't have to design your own life. Love and beauty and meaning won't desert you just because you let go of them. Look at the needs of the whole situation and take your cues from that."

So while my husband began sending out applications to programs around the country, I began looking around me at what I would be leaving behind. It was the beauty of New Mexico and my involvement with the Center that I would miss most.

That morning at the Center I opened the door that led to the big back lot and stepped out onto the wooden platform that is part of a wheelchair ramp built recently by one of the men at the Center. The sturdy feel of that platform under my feet filled me with a sense of well-being, and looking down I was captivated by the ruddy gold color of the lumber and the alignment of the nails in the wood. Was every wheelchair ramp this beautiful? Had I ever really seen one before?

I sat down on the wooden steps that led down to the grass and looked across at the picnic table under the cottonwoods. Made by another man at the Center, it had the same sturdy simplicity of love made solid and lasting and left unsigned among the other unsigned beauties of the yard—the cottonwoods, poplars, butterflies, and wildflowers.

A lot of potluck suppers have been spread out on that table, but it's still not an image of coziness to me. It's more akin to those tables where Jesus sat down to eat with the outcasts of Galilee and sent ripples of excitement through the countryside by virtue of his boldness and authenticity. The authenticity I've encountered among people here is more diffuse and less dramatic, worked out in many otherwise ordinary lives rather than concentrated in the startling personality of one person. But the effect is similar—real calling to real, risk enabling risk.

I had been coming to the Center for about a year, attending lectures and Sunday evening contemplative prayer sessions, when I signed up last July for a three-day workshop by Ched Myers on Nonviolence and the Gospel of Mark. About midway through the weekend I realized that I felt a deep resonance with the people in the room. Scott Peck has described this as one stage in the process of community formation, but I was surprised to encounter it in myself because I've usually avoided groups and preferred being with one person at a time. I had assumed that my community, if I ever had one, would be a collection of friendships made one at a time. Here were people whose company I probably would not seek out individually—yet in aggregate they made something available to me, some energy that carried me beyond myself like a great river carrying the outflow of many inland waterways out to sea.

When the workshop broke for lunch, I sat down at the picnic table next to Richard and he asked me if I'd like to get more involved with the Center. I was so deeply honored to be asked, and so afraid of being pulled off-center by that honor, that I said no, not now, I need to be smaller. But the pull of the river was strong, and by the next day that *no* was overwhelmed by the *yes* of something begging to be born. I found myself wandering around the house, unable to concentrate on the simplest chore, as distracted as a woman about to go into labor. Or someone falling in love.

My husband could tell something was going on and wondered where all this would lead. I wondered myself. Since this was not an interest he shared, he worried that it would come between us. I fell asleep one night fretting about it and woke up the next morning with this sentence in my head: "You may bloom at the Center for Action and Contemplation but you will always be rooted in Dan." I saw that the nurturing and challenging energy in one's life can come from different sources and still be complementary, like soil and sun in the life of a plant. As it turned out, this was the place where I found my voice.

I had written for newspapers on and off since I was in high school, but I didn't discover my own voice until I began writing for *Radical Grace* last year. Writing suddenly got easier—it no longer felt like chiseling words into stone or pulling my own teeth, but more like digging a private well and tapping into an underground aquifer; I was buoyed up by the ground water of other people's lives flowing into my own. But the real joy for me as a writer was not just making the water available but making it beautiful, directing it into pools where it could catch the light and shimmer with experience. I still have to dig the wells and design the pools, but the water flowing into them is pure gift, and it is gratitude for the gift that fuels the work.

So when I say that I found my own voice, what I really mean is that I found a voice that was not just my own, but one that used the particulars of my situation to come into being. It was my way of being in the Body of Christ.

And finding myself there, I no longer had to shuttle back and forth between self-actualization and self-effacement, as if I had to create my own life and then die to save it. Trying to do both had been like writing my name and then erasing it, which, as any first-grader knows, you can only do so many times before you make a hole in the paper. The resolution of this conflict turned out to be writing something other than my own name. I don't mean that I had to ignore my own story—I just had to stop thinking of it as the only one that mattered.

He must increase, but I must decrease, said John the Baptist of his relationship with Christ, and that's where it all comes together for me. It was in the process of writing that I came to understand something about increase and decrease.

The psychic energy that went into writing had to be withdrawn from somewhere else. As it turned out, it had already been withdrawn and was waiting to be used: It had been withdrawn from the pursuit of adventure and romance that had occupied my adult life before I had children. I was an actress in college, then worked as a photographer and a reporter, traveled a lot, and eventually went to medical school, thinking that that endeavor, surely, would satisfy my deepest desire to give myself completely to something, or someone, and lose myself in the process.

I was trying, instinctively, to save my life by losing it. But it kept coming back. At some point in every career I would find myself on center stage feeling somehow false and inauthentic, in danger of doing for applause what I had done originally for pleasure, worried about settling for a career instead of a vocation. At that point I always wanted to start over so that I could be invisible again. My passion for travel and for new beginnings, I realize now, was really a passion for stripping away the constraints of a role. It was also a way of avoiding responsibility.

Family life has been a good antidote for that, because it's no longer a question of leaving and starting over; and there's no point in asking whether something is done for pleasure or applause because it's usually neither and it has to get done anyway.

On the other hand, being at home with small children was the closest I ever came to getting a hole rubbed clean through my paper, so to speak, by the demands that every mother knows well. But this was the first situation I could not leave, and that proved to be a great boon; because instead of looking over the rainbow for a way out, I had to look to myself, and that is when my own voice opened up, both as a way out of my own isolation at home and a way into life at a deeper level.

What family life contributed to that voice was, in retrospect, a genuine and salutory decrease in me—a decrease into ordinariness that turned out to be exactly the kind of long-term invisibility I needed. In this ordinariness my life mingled with other people's enough for their voices to enter mine; and mine gathered strength from theirs like melting snow in the mountains gathers force from other streams and rivers on its way down. The decrease of the interesting person allowed for the increase of the writer.

While I had been sitting on the wooden steps, the sun had climbed to a spot directly overhead and the shadows had receded. The lovely old cottonwoods stood in the middle of their dark green pools of shade, and two of them together formed a canopy over the picnic table. The Center's dedication Mass last summer came to mind—it was held out here under the cottonwoods on the feast of John the Baptist, and one of the songs we sang had this refrain:

> We are the boat, we are the sea,
> I sail in you, you sail in me.

A great sadness washed over me as I thought about what I had found here and what I would have to leave so soon. But the image of the great river carrying all of us along comforted me. I realized that the river that had pulled me out of myself and into life was not one that I would ever have to leave, because it was really just a way of being in the world. It was this way of being that gave me my voice, and this was the voice that could say, "Yes, I can go."

Is This "Women Stuff" Important?

RICHARD ROHR, OFM

> Throughout the earth men spoke the same language, with the same vocabulary. . . . But they said to one another, "Come, let us build ourselves a town and a tower with its top reaching heaven." *Gen. 11:1, 4*

> In the world the powerful lord it over the others. . . . This must not happen among you. *Luke 22:25, 26*

We would probably not have to ask the question in our title if we had understood the lessons in these two scriptures. Our title is the question of a male, who is also white, educated, middle-class, and even priestly. Each of these perspectives makes it less likely that I would be aware of "women stuff," much less see any problems or need to change anything. We white males have been holding all the cards, naming all the questions, and providing all the answers for the entire Christian era—except for those few golden years when God took poor flesh in Jesus. He took twelve Jewish men and tried to show them how they could be part of the solution instead of part of the problem. Unfortunately, it didn't work. Males continued to build towers and operate as lords over others, and women stuff just didn't fit in. That is the world and the church that I was born into. It is preoccupied with domination and status quo logic to this day and thus finds itself largely incapable of understanding (much less believing) most of the clear teachings of Jesus. Poverty, meekness or nonviolence, tears, justice-love, mercy, purity of heart, peacemaking and reconciliation, bearing persecution or what we might call "losing graciously" are his opening statements. But try to get elected in a Christian country or promoted to a Catholic bishopric today while taking those teachings seriously! Yet Jesus forthrightly called them the Eight Happinesses.

Apparently, Christian men of power have decided that happiness is optional. What is mandatory and necessary it that the world be divided into those who have the power and those who don't. It makes for good order, at least for those on top, and order is more important than happiness. Our word for this addictive view of reality is *patriarchy,* which means the "rule of the fathers." It is the basis of all major relational systems in the Western world. In the patriarchal view (1) all relationships are eventually defined in terms of superiority and inferiority, and (2) the all-important need for order and control is assured by the exercise of dominative power. Now that does not sound so bad if the status quo happens to be working in your favor. But it has served to dehumanize and therefore despiritualize generations of races, nations, professions, women, sexual minorities, handicapped people, the weak, and the elderly whom the powerful are able to disparage culturally and dismiss as "of no account." Not only are the rich and powerful able to project their own darkness onto such groups, but the groups normally accept that darkness as their true value. The utter evil of such patriarchy is that both the oppressor and the oppressed are incapable of real spiritual growth. The powerful, by rejecting their shadow, are hopelessly inflated. The powerless, by receiving others' shadows, are endlessly deflated. Both lose. And that is why patriarchy is evil.

Patriarchy is the nerve center of an entire worldview that idealizes winning over others, power and control (the outer face of fear), and the much-abused philosophies of "might makes right" and "peace through strength." Without "success" (by his own definition) and control the patriarch does not know who he is. Many would honestly admit that life would not be worth living, which shows how deep the addiction has become. We must readily admit that many women are also patriarchs in this sense, or at least codependent members of the male system. They will often defend the system even more feverishly than many males: Witness Margaret Thatcher, Nancy Reagan, and Imelda Marcos!

The language of patriarchy is always a noble or macho language of patriotism and freedom. Men (and their female echoes) are always speaking it, but the amazing thing is that anyone is still willing to believe it. Among other places where it is obviously spoken today are Beirut, Belfast, Moscow, Johannesburg, San Salvador, Washington, and Jerusalem. But fortunately the poor, the oppressed and marginalized, and especially women are beginning to trust their natural and truly religious instincts. In some cases this leads them to mistrust and even disobey the cerebral and self-assured conclusions of the powers that be. You might call that arrogance and pride. You might also call it courage. Or sometimes even faith. God will sort it out; I don't have to. Remember, I'm learning to give up my need for control and explanation!

We have to move toward the instinctual point, since left-brain reason and logic have served us so poorly at this point in Western civilization. We find ourselves satisfied with two-thirds of our people either starving, unemployed, or homeless, while unthinkingly polluting and preparing to bomb the rest—and at the same time touting glorious phrases like freedom, free enterprise, "making the world safe for democracy," and "our sacred family values." Man's capacity to disguise his own darkness seems endless. Patriarchal logic is only logic in favor of the system and status quo—which is proudly called "the real world." Believe me, because I always hear it quoted to me after my sermons, usually from polite men in three-piece suits: "That was an interesting talk there 'Father,' but you know, in the real world. . . ." The fathers of the system hate nothing more than another father who refuses the rules of the game.

That is precisely our role in proclaiming the new system that Jesus called the Reign of God. That's why he trained the twelve men to think and act in a new way. It's sort of a subversion-from-within tactic, but since we have not done very well at it, God is now sending the women to help us. "Women stuff" is the hidden energy behind almost all of the justice issues. The movement toward nonviolence and disarmament, homelessness and refugee problems, the raping of the earth and its resources, sexual and physical abuse issues, the idolatry of profit and the corporation, and the rejection of the poor will not move beyond the present impasse until the underlying issues of power, prestige, and possessions are exposed for the lie that they are. Under the new Russian perestroika or "restructuring," we are finally seeing beyond the artificial enemies to the real problem. Surprisingly, we are seeing that the power elites under communism are just as opposed to change as are the wealthy and powerful under capitalism. Do you see what that tells us? Russia and communism are not the final enemy; powerful domination in every system wants to maintain its privilege. As the Berlin Wall was about to be destroyed, we learned that half of the people in West Berlin in fact did not want it torn down! I'll bet I can tell you which half; those who put their identity and security in the economic system. So also, maleness is not the problem, but male pretensions of power and winning. These towers of Babel have cost men their own souls for too long—along with the bodies, spirits, and dignity of much of the rest of the world.

Pyramids are always pyramids of sacrifice. Whether it is the hundreds of thousands of slaves creating monuments to Egyptian kings, the sacrificial victims offering their hearts to Aztec gods, or the underpaid maids and janitors in the tourist hotels of the world, someone always has to give his life or her life so that someone else can be "special." When that specialness is idealized and protected, instead of avoided and made unnecessary as Jesus taught, we have the destructive and dark side of power. Jesus struck at the nerve center of all of these when he empowered honest human relationships instead of degrees of religious worthiness. Jesus built circles instead of pyramids. What they could not forgive him for, even on the cross, was that he announced the necessary destruction of the holy temple. "Not a stone will stand on a stone. Everything will be destroyed" (Mark 13:2). He knew that the temple, now divided into courts of worthiness, was not a place where God was first as much as a place that kept the central storehouse economy in control and the widow with her "mite" outside. Thus he revealingly called it "the treasury" (Mark 12:41) and committed the unforgivable sin of overturning the tables of "those who were selling and buying there" (Matt. 21:12). In attacking the temple, he attacked Judaism's final tower and democratized religion once and for all. But like Aaron the first priest, we priests have been building golden calves and golden temples ever since. With priests and minister, the assumption is that if it is good for religion, it is good for God. "False!" said Jesus.

Even the tower of Babel incident referred to at the beginning of this article reveals that God had to scatter and confuse the one language of the men who had built the pretentious tower "to make a name for ourselves" (Gen. 11:4). Here we have the anomaly of a God who separates and divides people when they have structured themselves wrongly. In an early style of perestroika, God reverses this process at Pentecost when tongues of fire now unite the different languages into one universal language of the Spirit, so that "each hears in their own language about the wonderful works of God" (Acts 2:11). Circles of communication, networks of nations, true brotherhood and sisterhood are finally possible in this new people who are born of God's Spirit. And it is no accident that God the Spirit is presented in a feminine and maternal image from which we are "born" (John 3:5–8). Immediately after the giving of the Pentecost Spirit we have the further birth of real and honest community: "The faithful all lived together and owned everything in common; they sold their goods and possessions and shared out of the proceeds according to each one's need" (Acts 2:44–45). We can only imagine this fondly since it has rarely happened again. Francis of Assisi tried. The vow of poverty was an attempt. But the patriarchal need for domination and possession preferred towers and basilicas to human community, degrees of worthiness instead of honest human relationships. Dare I list the line-up? Pope, Curia, Cardinals, Metropolitans, Archbishops, Bishops, Vicars, General, Monsignors, Priests, Deacons, Subdeacons, (recently abolished as unnecessary!), Exorcists, Acolytes, Lectors, and Porters constitute the *cleros* or "separated ones." If there is any worthiness left, it is graciously dispensed to the *laos,* the 99 percent of the membership who are told exactly how they can be worthy. Forgive my sarcasm, but it is intentional and long overdue. God's reputation is at stake.

The feminine insight is a rediscovery of Jesus' spirit, a reemergence of a well-suppressed truth, and eventual political upheaval, a certain reform of our hearing of the Gospel and someday perhaps the very structures of the churches—and all proceeding from a "knowing" in the mother's womb; exactly where we received Christ for the first time.

It was no accident that we Catholics had a psychological need to exalt Mary to the role of a goddess. I am not sure whether it was an inherent need to balance ourselves, a disguise for the patriarchy underneath, a love affair with the denied woman within, or just a work of the Spirit, but it is an overwhelming example of instinct winning out over logic and theology. So much so, in fact, that the only two infallible statements of this Roman patriarchal church are ironically the assumption of the physical body of Mary into heaven and her privileged choice and protection by God called the "Immaculate Conception." Furthermore, we even celebrate her "Coronation as Queen of heaven and earth." I'm really all for it, but none of these are found in Scripture or public revelation. Amazing how this male church was always feminist—and unwittingly ready to bend all the rules to say so! That healthy instinct has now come to our service and we call it "women stuff." Sorry, boys, we Catholics have always been there. Proud and orthodox in public, but Mama's boys whenever we could find an excuse for it. It's not new or liberal or dangerous; it's very old, quite conservative, and as traditional as Mary and the eight Beatitudes.

The feminist insight explains the vast majority of Jesus' teachings, a male acting very differently in an almost totally patriarchal Jewish society. Like Mary, the church also has "treasured these things in her heart" (Luke 2:19). Only in time are they ready to come forth, like Jesus from her womb. Jesus would never have broken through as the fresh Word of the Father if he had, for example, acted nonviolently in a feminine body. It would not have been Divine Revelation because we expect and demand that *women* be patient, nurturing, forgiving, healing, self-effacing, and self-sacrificing. Women are expected to be nonviolent in a violent male society (look at our one-sided attitude toward rape, adultery, physical abuse, and, in many cultures, divorce), but we are still not prepared for males, institutions, or nations to act nonviolently.

That is why God had to become incarnate for us in the body of a man. Unfortunately, we kept the name and image of Jesus to exalt male leadership but basically rejected most of Jesus' teachings as impractical and unreasonable in the pyramidal "real world" of church and state—as indeed they are! We conveniently fit Jesus back into our more practical way of being a religious institution— and lost most of his unique and revolutionary strategy for dealing with human evil. Now we find ourselves helpless and without the tools to deal with war, greed, and the endless whimsy of the individual ego.

No one was wicked or intentional in all of this, nor is it all wrong and lost, but it does show the depth and disguise of evil. Power is surely not intrinsically wrong, but it is very dangerous and, in my opinion, only spiritually mature people can handle it. Power, another word for the Spirit in Scripture, is most effective when it is clearly recognized as such and clearly shared as a common but diverse gift. At Pentecost the Spirit came down on "all" (Acts 2:1), giving them the power to recognize and affirm life within themselves and in one another. That is the richest meaning of authority. It is the power to author life in others. That power is not exclusively or even primarily held by men. It seems to me that should be rather self-evident. At the present moment of history unbalanced male consciousness has given us both totalitarian communism and greedy capitalism, neither of which seeks the common good of humanity. The are both pyramids of sacrifice and both afraid of circles of truth and justice.

I see nothing in the New Testament that tells me that Jesus intended or desired his new community to be modeled on the power structures of the Roman Empire. I further see nothing in the life narrative of Peter the fisherman that tells me that he can be expected to do anything but doubt, bungle, deny, and run. But he also professes love and stands as a full prophetic image of the de facto life of the hierarchy and the church. Jesus' love of Peter tells me that Jesus is willing to work with just such human brokenness— just as he is willing to work with all of the rest of the world that is unsuitable, out of order, unorthodox, and even sinful. That unfortunately, is what patriarchy is unwilling and unable to do. It demands an infallible pope and a "worthy" people. The love of power does not have the capacity to nurture anything that it cannot explain or control. The exclusive rule of the fathers not only makes community and justice impossible but also holds Christ's salvation at the level of salvation theories and techniques that educated clerics can be "right" about. The starving millions deserve a better God than that. They deserve the Father that Jesus knew. The Father that Jesus knew looks amazingly like what most cultures would call "Mother." In Luke 15, the story of the prodigal son, Jesus makes his most complete presentation of the character of this Father, whom he called God. The father is in every way the total opposite of the male patriarch and even rejects his older son's appeal to a world of worthiness and merit. He not only allows the younger son to make choices against him but even empowers him to do so by giving him the money! After his bad mistakes, the father still refuses his right to restore order or impose a penance, even though the prodigal son offers to serve as a hired servant. Both his leaving and his returning are treated as necessary but painful acts of adult freedom. In every way he can, the father makes mutuality and vulnerability possible. As Sr. Sandra Schneiders says, this new kind of father "refuses to own us, demand our submission, or punish our rebellion. Father God is one who respects our freedom, mourns our alienation, waits patiently for our return, and accepts our love as pure gift. . . . God tries to educate the older brother, and through him all disciples who prefer the security of law to the adventure of grace." In an absolutely reeling conclusion, she states that the "power God refuses to assume over us is surely not given by God to any human being." Not even to the church, which must always live in the image of the heavenly Father.

All this "women stuff" is not only important, it is the other half of conversion, the other half of salvation, the other half of wholeness that completes God's work of art. I believe this mystery is imaged in the Woman of the twelfth chapter of the Book of Revelation: "pregnant, and in labor, crying aloud in the pangs of childbirth . . . and finally escaping into the desert until her time."

Could this be the time? I think it must be. The world is tired of Pentagons and pyramids, empires and corporations that only abort God's child. The East has stopped playing the other half of our game and now speaks disturbingly of glasnost and perestroika. The West is alive with liberation movements at every level of consciousness, with race, gender, and economic (prestige, power, and possessions!) issues at the forefront. Even the church is finding the humility to recognize its fear of the subjective and the personal and its unlawful marriage to the systems of power and control. The woman is coming out of her desert escape, with no possibility of return. Too many of us have seen her gift. The Holy Child Wisdom is among us and the vision is compelling. We *can* live and think differently.

Yes; this "women stuff" is very important—more than this white male priest ever imagined or desired! My God was too small and too male. Now I don't know how to fight with a woman. What I, what we, need to learn is to make love to Her, to recognize and affirm Her gifts, to understand that She is intrinsic to divine and human wholeness.

Pursued by the Love
That Casts Out Fear

LINDA HARDY

I was sitting stiffly on the edge of the examining table facing an elderly obstetrician who looked tired but unhurried as the late afternoon sun slanted into his office. "So you're determined not to carry this pregnancy?" he asked.

"Yes," I replied.

It was the spring of my junior year in college and abortion was still illegal. When I discovered that I was pregnant, my boyfriend wanted to get married. I said no. He then asked me to have the baby and give it to him. I said no.

My world had suddenly grown constricted and all I wanted was a way out. Abortion was the only thing I considered. As it turned out, it was done in a hospital as a routine "D and C" (dilation and curettage) by a doctor who charged nothing. When he asked at a follow-up visit if I had any qualms about it, I said no.

How that *no* has changed over the years is the story of my spiritual journey, a journey that began with the question, "What do I want?" and eventually led me to ask instead, "Lord, what would you have of me?" Recently, the dramatic healing of an abortion that occurred nineteen years ago—and which I long believed needed no healing—changed the question to "How do you want to love me, Jesus?"

The focus had shifted from the love I could give to the love I could only surrender to. That surrender turned out to be my empowerment, and that empowerment is what allows me now to come out of my foxhole in the abortion war.

I can do that only because I have experienced the love that casts our fear. I don't mean that I've become fearless. I mean that all kinds of anxieties have fled like birds of prey, leaving me under the clear blue sky of this certain knowledge: The purpose of my life is to bear witness to the love I have received.

Now as a witness I can only speak about what I know firsthand, what I myself have seen. Some of what I see at this point is contradictory, but I can't pretend I don't see it.

When I look at the abortion, for example, I see it from two perspectives: then and now. What I see now amplifies what I saw then, but doesn't cancel it out.

The morning I entered the hospital, a middle-aged woman in admitting saw I was underage and told me I needed parental permission for any procedure. "My mother's dead and I don't want to upset my father," I told her. A look of recognition flashed between us and she immediately changed from pleasant functionary to committed ally, eventually discovering that the doctor could get me in by certifying my case as an emergency. He did.

Now it is possible to see this man as a liar and a murderer and the woman in admitting as his accomplice. It is also possible to see how they might have felt some responsibility for a woman who, if turned away, might resort to more dangerous means to achieve the same end. I believe they were responding in good faith to the promptings of their own conscience, and that concern for a woman they could see took precedence over concern for a five-week-old fetus they could not see.

When I emerged from the hospital the next morning, I felt like someone who had made it to freedom on an underground railway—all I could feel was gratitude toward those who had stepped out of the shadows to help me. It would be years before I could see the hidden reality in that experience—the life that was lost so that my own life could proceed undisturbed.

In the meantime, I could not understand the anguish other women described over a choice I myself had made without hesitation. A neighbor once told me that abortion was so abhorrent to her and the alternative so impossible that she had driven out to a lake to commit suicide. But as she sat on the bank she was stopped by this thought; "If I do this, I'm taking two lives. Abortion would take only one."

At a Catholic Worker House in New York City I met a middle-aged Italian woman whose skin was raw from compulsive hand-washing, the Lady Macbeth way of dealing with guilt. "As God is my witness," she told me with pleading in her voice, "I did not have an abortion."

My own change of heart never led me to such extremes. It began several years after college, when I was abandoning my basically happy but shallow life in search of something deeper. I began listening more attentively to my own heart.

During that time I was working odd hours as a newspaper photographer and spending much of my time off sitting in empty churches, waiting and listening. I was often moved to tears, not by any identifiable sadness but simply by the feeling that some deep part of me had been touched.

Meanwhile, abortion has been legalized and the outcry over it was mounting. One afternoon I heard on the radio that the church had condemned abortion "even in cases of incest or rape."

"That's outrageous," I thought. But because I was in a listening mode, I could hear a small voice inside me ask, "How is it not a life?"

It was a sincere question from that part of me which was just coming to life. Since I couldn't answer it to my satisfaction, I had to go on to harder questions: "If a fetus is a human life, is it less so because of the circumstances under which it was conceived? Is someone's status as a human being dependent on the goodwill of other people?"

Around that time I decided to go to confession. In a traditional confessional a priest told me that abortion was a "reserved sin" and so he needed permission from the bishop to forgive it.* I came back in three days, as he'd instructed, and learned absolution had

---

*NOTE: In many dioceses in our country the bishop gives his priests the faculty to remit this censure in the Sacrament of Reconciliation.

been granted. Some minor penance was given, the confessional window clicked shut, and I went back to sitting alone in church.

But my own journey was just beginning. Intellectually, I could acknowledge my wrongdoing, but my heart was still not engaged. Suspecting that I might be repressing something, I prayed for an experience of true sorrow. For more than ten years nothing happened.

Then several years ago I was seized by an attack of scrupulosity over the way I'd treated someone in the past. I went to confession, but my guilt was so out of proportion to the deed that the priest made further inquiries. We were facing each other in a small room, and when I mentioned the abortion, he asked if I had ever prayed through it with anyone. I hadn't, so we began right there.

"Did you ever have any sense of it as a girl or boy?" he asked.

"A girl," I said.

Can you give her name?"

"Anne," I said.

Much of the "praying through" had to do with forgiveness—forgiving anyone who had hurt me in connection with the abortion (I said no one had) and asking forgiveness of anyone I had hurt, including the child. It was at that point that my prayers for true repentance were answered and the floodgates of my tears were opened. Having tapped into the depth of gratitude I felt for my own life, I saw the enormity of what I had denied someone else.

"But how can I ask forgiveness of someone for not allowing them life?" I cried.

"Just do it," he said.

That encounter initiated a deep healing but also created more problems for me. Ever since I'd started asking, "How is it not a life?" I'd had the feeling that I was being led into dangerous territory. For one thing, I was breaking rank with close friends by the question I had to ask: "If the fetus is a person, shouldn't its life be protected by law?"

Yet if I really believed that, why did I duck out of church one Sunday to avoid the woman gathering signatures for a constitutional amendment against abortion?

My trouble was that I could not tune anyone out. I could not call one side ludicrous for believing that life begins at conception, nor could I call the other side murderers for believing otherwise. I felt that my position was the most untenable of all: I myself had come to regard the unborn child as a person, but I balked at outlawing abortion. I attributed that to moral cowardice.

To complicate matters, I had the uneasy feeling that my personal history required something of me and I dreaded to think what it might be. In my worst-case scenario, I would have to sit outside an abortion clinic, somehow conveying the message: "I had an abortion myself. I would not call you a murderer. If you would like to talk . . ."

I didn't want to do that and so I wondered, "Am I like Jonah refusing to preach repentance to Nineveh?" I feared that some life circumstance would swallow me up like a whale and send me right back to the situation I most wanted to avoid. That is in fact what happened.

What drew me into the belly of the whale was another attack of scrupulosity that prompted me to sit down and ask, "Why am I feeling so bad about this when I've done things so much worse?"

What came next was the feeling that I was in the presence of Anne, and my dread began rising. But the urgency of that presence could not be ignored. I felt that I was somehow "seeing" her—not seeing her physical features, but looking into her heart and seeing her disposition toward me.

After a long time of looking, I realized that there was not a shred of condemnation there. Coming back at me as I looked was only wave upon wave of unconditional love.

"But if love is *here,*" I thought with growing amazement, "where is love *not?*"

All debts were canceled, I realized, and all ledgers lost. All watertight argument had burst and love was coming in through all the doors and windows. God was indeed pursuing me, it seemed, but only to say: *"Nothing is required."* And that made me want to give everything.

Washed up on the shores of Nineveh, I was exhilarated to discover that I was finally free of the fear that had dogged me for so long—the fear of any apparent inconsistency and moral cowardice. I do not say that I am free of such things, but only that I do not fear them. To bear witness to the love that has saturated my being, I have to hold up for view the whole ragged cloth of my life.

When love cast out fear, it left in its place this joy: I can speak the truth of my own experience. I do not have to join any group in which the voices coming from my own heart will be shouted down if I am to listen to the voice that asks, "How is it not a life?" then I must also listen to the voice that asks, "Is the law the best way to bear witness to life?"

When I wanted an abortion, the law did not stop me. When I wanted to avoid the issue altogether, my course was changed by the love that cast out fear. That is why I believe love is stronger than law.

Law creates adversaries, love reconciles. The law produced prosecutors and defendants, all arguing ferociously that part of the truth which advances their case. Love allows for mutual surrender and it is only in that context, I believe, that the whole truth can be seen.

I see the abortion war being fought from the tops of two mountains. From one mountain comes the cry, "It's a woman's body!" and from the other, "It's a child's life!" I can't see how it's not both, and that is why my own path through Nineveh lies in the valley between those two mountains. That route may be indefensible, but I'm not defending anything. I'm bearing witness to a love that makes no sense—the love that came into my life by way of my gravest sin. For that task, total exposure is better than armor.

Abortion is being argued in all kinds of public places, but the decision to have an abortion, or attempt one, is made by individual women responding to the pressures of their own situation. A woman feeling trapped and fearful is not likely to choose life. What saves the lives of women and children is the same thing that redeems lives—the love that casts out fear.

Pious Mirth:
A New Year Meditation

KENT SMITH

*A*s we approach the turn of the year and the Center's theme of reconstruction, some of us will see the New Year as offering unbounded opportunities. Others will see only confirmation that little is new except the renewal of old miseries.

In large measure, what we bring to the year is what we expect from it. The preacher of the Old Testament said: "What has been is what will be, and what has been done is what will be done and there is nothing new under the sun." I would rather look to the joyous words of the last verse of Luther's Christmas hymn:

> Glory to God in Highest Heaven
> Who unto man his son hath given,
> While angels sing with pious mirth
> A glad New Year to all the earth.

If angels can look to the New Year, singing greeting with pious mirth, why can't we?

Pious and *mirth* are both old-fashioned words. We do not commonly describe people as being pious today—maybe religious or spiritual, but seldom pious. Nor do we talk about mirth—happiness or having fun, but not mirth. Mirth is defined as happiness or gaiety as shown by, or accompanied with, laughter, merriment, jollity. It is not just an inner feeling of joy or just an outward expression of laughter, it is both. Like a sacrament, it is an outward expression of an inner grace.

But what is pious mirth? To be pious is to manifest devotion to God, to be zealous in prayer or acts of worship. Piety and mirth don't seem to belong together. Although angels are said to sing with pious mirth, does it have anything to do with us? Yet angels sing to "all the earth." We should be able to understand pious mirth.

There is a kind of piety that excludes mirth. The Puritans in New England had little use for pleasure of any kind. Christmas was outlawed as a pagan festival; dancing around a May pole was a criminal offense; peace and happiness were to come from hard work and worship of God. Piety was its own reward. These pious persons knew they were right; they knew they worked hard; they hoped God would bless them. Indeed, the success of hard work was often equated with God's blessing. Those less successful were seen as the unfaithful, the unchosen part of humanity, worthy of contempt. This was piety without mirth.

But mirth without piety can be equally unsatisfactory. Those who pursue pleasure for its own sake, seek to have fun at the expense of others, recognize no sense of the tragic, fritter life away, seeking one thrill after another—such people eventually end up looking and feeling as unhappy as the Puritans.

Both groups miss the balance; they miss the tension between piety and mirth.

Pious mirth means having one's life rooted in those serious ultimate questions of human existence which are found in religion, spirituality, philosophical inquiry, and existential searching. There are no absolute answers. But to struggle honestly with the questions of who I am, where I am going, and what it all means is to develop an often neglected dimension of what it is to be human.

This is not to suggest that we struggle in some existential abyss. it is a struggle shared with others—and being with others is the first dimension of mirth. A truly shared activity must have some pleasure, some joy, some anticipation of accomplishment built into it. When people work and struggle together, they will find ways to celebrate together. The inner feelings of joy will find outward expression in a meal, a drink, a dance, a celebration, a festival, a sacrament. Pious mirth is rooted in real concern and understanding of ourselves and others, reaching beyond itself to celebrate with others the meaning and love we can affirm in spite of the world around us and the pain within us. This brings lasting joy.

On Death and Rebirth

CHRISTINA SPAHN

"*I*t was good while it lasted." The words surprised me in a way one is surprised who realizes a new sense of self after having said more that was consciously intended. The setting was the CAC staff's weekly check-in session at which we reflect together on issues and events of our personal lives, and the topic was our relationship with the church.

For most of my life I've been a church "insider"—or so I thought: educated primarily in Catholic schools, a member of a religious community for twenty-one years, degreed in theology and ministry, employed in parochial school, parish, and archdiocesan work. I knew and worked well within the system. In return, I was affirmed in a self-image that identified very strongly with that system. This doesn't mean there weren't questions and conflicts. There were, but *we* would work things out and move toward a future bright with promise. Meanwhile, I committed considerable energy to that working-out process.

Five years ago, in a period of personal upheaval and trauma that I've since identified as grace, my thinking began to change. In regard to my community, the inner disparity between *we* and *I* had grown so wide that it could no longer be ignored. *We* did not seem much inclined to grapple with changes that seemed essential to my life, but *I* realized not only that I could but that I must.

Leaving my community was the most painful thing I've ever done; it's also been the most life-giving. The questions and conflicts that initiated the process are still with me: What does Christian discipleship in today's world demand? How are Gospel values to be enfleshed in my life? To whom are the evangelical counsels addressed, and what do they mean today? What are the unique gifts of the feminine and how can I best use them? To what does love of God and neighbor call me, and how can I respond? What areas of my life are most in need of conversion?

The sense of personal responsibility for dealing with these questions has at times been frightening. But there's also been an awareness of peace, integrity, and trust in a loving God who, as Merton prays, "will lead me by the right road though I may know nothing about it."

It is perhaps the urgency of these questions that led me during that staff check-in to an articulated awareness that my relationship with the church is no longer what it once was. Nor does it need to be! There is much about the church that saddens me: its concern for power and control, its treatment of women, the pain occasioned by its ostrich-like approach to sexuality, its failure to live radically the message it proclaims, its willingness to sacrifice its eucharistic tradition at the altar of celibacy, its clericalism and enthronement of the masculine, its failure to call its members compassionately and energetically to lives of justice, its present unwillingness to consider institutional conversion and reform.

Yet, even in stating the above, I recognize that the sense of distance I feel is not from the church at large or from the church of history but from that highly visible segment of the church which, in its frenetic desire for institutional maintenance, is most effectively destroying the structures it seeks to preserve. That church is dying, and the fact that those who would preserve it are doing the most to further its demise only illustrates the blindness occasioned by too readily confusing what has been with what needs to be.

Meanwhile, though, even as the church dies, it is also coming to birth: in the *comunidades de base* of the Third World, in the planetary struggle for justice and stewardship, in Catholic Workers houses and vigils for peace, in the prayerful reading of Scripture and contemplative sitting, in sacramental celebration but also in celebration of a sacramental world, in the persistence of women and men who recognize the church's need to discover and affirm the feminine, to ask the hard questions, and to live in a state of continual conversion.

Finally, it seems to me that the church is born in the lives of those, who, gifted, graced, and nourished to maturity in a Catholicism now passing, no longer feel as "at home" as they once did. Caught between the now and not-yet, searching, waiting, turning to Scripture and each other, these individuals enflesh the church into the future.

Center and Circumference

RICHARD ROHR, OFM

> Turning and turning in the widening gyre
> The falcon cannot hear the falconer;
> Things fall apart; the center cannot hold;
> Mere anarchy is loosed upon the world,
> The blood-dimmed tide is loosed,
> and everywhere
> The ceremony of innocence is drowned;
> The best lack of all conviction, while the worst
> Are full of passionate intensity.
> William Butler Yeats, *"The Second Coming"*

We are a circumference people, with little access to the Center. We live on the boundaries of our own lives, "in the widening gyre," confusing edges with essence, too quickly claiming the superficial as substance. As Yeats predicted, things have fallen apart, "the center cannot hold."

If the circumferences of our lives were evil, they would be easier to moralize about. But boundaries and edges are not bad as much as they are passing accidental, sometimes illusory, too often in need of defense and decoration. Our skin is not bad; it's just not our soul. But "skin" might also be the only beginning point available to a modern age, freed from the limitations and sufferings that forced most earlier peoples to an inner place of refuge. We remain on the circumference of our soul for so long, it seems like life. Not many people are telling us there is anything more. And maybe the confusion lies even deeper. We have always looked for the soul *inside* the body. Perhaps our bodies are merely a part of a much larger Soul. I think that is exactly what the wisdom tradition is saying.

Let's presume there was an earlier age when people had easy and natural access to their soul. I am not sure if this age ever existed any more than did the Garden of Eden, where all was naked and in harmony; but if it did, it consisted of people who were either loved very well at their Center or who suffered very much on their surface—probably both. The rest of us have to rediscover and return to the Garden by an arduous route. This movement *back* to Paradise is the blood, guts, and history of the whole Bible. It is both an awakening and a quieting, a passion for and a surrendering to, a caring and a not caring. It is both Center and circumference, and I am not in charge of either one. But I have to begin somewhere. For most of us the beginning point is on the edges. Yet the teachers tell us not to stay there! The movement beyond is called conversion, integration, or holiness. It feels more and more like a divine trick, if you try to resolve it in your head. So let's go somewhere else.

Less than a block from my house in downtown Albuquerque, there is a sidewalk where the homeless often sit against the wall to catch the morning sun. A few days ago, I saw new graffiti chalked clearly on the pavement. It touched me so profoundly that I immediately went home and wrote it in my journal. It said, "I watch how foolishly man guards his nothing, thereby keeping us out. Truly God is hated here." I can only guess at what kind of person wrote such wisdom, but I heard a paraphrase of Jesus in mind: "The people of the sidewalk might well be at the Center, and the people in their houses might well be on the circumference" (Luke 13:30, Mark 10:31, Matt. 19:30, 20:16). Now I can probably assume that this street person is not formally educated in theology or trained in contemplative spirituality. Yet from the edges, this person has clearly understood all that I am trying to say. Did she go through healing? Did he pay for psychotherapy? How does this person so clearly recognize the false nature of our self-image and yet the clear sense of being included and excluded? This street person has both edges and essence and also knows exactly who God is! You don't resolve the question in your head. The body is probably a better beginning point. It's in the soul, remember.

Living in this material world, with a physical body and in a culture of affluence that rewards the outer self, it is both more difficult to know our spiritual self and all the more necessary. Our skin-encapsulated egos are the only self that we know and therefore our only beginning place. But they are not the only or even the best place. That is our contemporary dilemma: 1) Our culture no longer values the inner journey. 2) We actively avoid and fear it. 3) In most cases we no longer even have the tools to go inward because, 4) we are enamored of and entrapped in the private ego and its private edges. In such culture, "the center cannot hold," at least for long.

How do you find what is supposedly already there? Why isn't it obvious? How do you awaken the Center? By thinking about it? By praying and meditating? By more silence and solitude? Yes, perhaps, but mostly by *living*—and living consciously. The edges suffered and enjoyed lead us back to the Center. The street person feels cold and rejection and has to go to a deeper place for warmth. The hero pushes against his own self-interested edges and finds that they don't matter. The alcoholic woman recognizes how she has hurt her family and breaks through to a compassion beyond her. In each case, the edges suffer, inform, partially self-destruct, and all are found to be unnecessary and even part of the problem. That which feels the pain also lets it go, and the Center stands revealed and sufficient! We do not find our own Center; it finds us. The body is in the soul. It is both the place of contact and the place of surrender. We don't think ourselves into a new way of living. We live ourselves into a new way of thinking. The journeys around the circumference lead us to life at the Center. Then by what is certainly a vicious and virtuous circle the Center calls all the journeys at the circumference into question! The ruthless ambition of the businessman can lead him to the very failure and emptiness that is the point of his conversion. Is the ambition therefore good or evil? Do we really have to sin to know salvation? Call me a "sin mystic," but that is exactly what I see happening in all my pastoral experience.

That does not mean that we should set out intentionally to sin. We only see the pattern after the fact. Julian of Norwich put it perfectly: "Commonly, first we fall and later we see it—and both are the Mercy of God." Wow! How did we ever lose that? It got hidden away in that least celebrated but absolutely central Easter Vigil service, when the deacon sings to the church about a *felix culpa*, the happy fault that precedes and necessitates the eternal Christ. Like all great mysteries of faith, it is hidden except to those who keep vigil and listen.

The overwhelming problem today is that people are creating and letting go of boundaries who have no hint of their own psychological or theological Center. Those who create boundaries often end up with hardened and defended edges, without permeability for others to move in or out. They may become either racists afraid of the "not-me" or codependents manipulating the world to meet their love and security needs. Those who too easily let go of boundaries will seek their soul forever outside themselves: She will make me happy. I need him for my sense of self. This church is who I am.

Those who have firmed up their own edges too quickly without finding their essential Center will be the enemies of ecumenism, forgiveness, vulnerability, and peacemaking between nations and classes. Those who let go of their edges too easily often pride themselves on their openness and tolerance. But even here there is both virtue and vice. The tolerance of the believer, rooted in God, is certainly the voice of wisdom; but the quick tolerance of the skeptic is largely meaningless, usually no more than a need to be liked. The first is the authentic lover, the faith-based prophet, the grounded agent of change; the second is a "born yesterday" believer, the eclectic liberal, the faddish New Ager. Unfortunately, the second is much more common on the American scene today, even in churches and social justice circles. We have our work to do.

The greatest gift of centered and surrendered people is that they know themselves as part of a larger history, a larger Self. In that sense, centered people are profoundly conservative, knowing that they only stand on the shoulders of their ancestors and will be another shoulder for the generation to come. Yet they are paradoxically open and reformist, because they have no private agendas or self-interest to protect. People who have learned to live from their Center know which boundaries are worth maintaining and which can be surrendered. Both reflect an obedience. If you want a litmus test for truly centered people, that's it: they are always free to obey.

Probably the most obvious indication of non-centered ec-centric people is that they are a pain to live with! Every ego boundary must be defended, negotiated, glorified: My reputation, my nation, my job, my religion, and even my ball team are really all I have to tell myself that I am somebody. No wonder wisdom, understanding, and community have come upon hard times!

Toward the end of his career Carl Jung said that he was not aware of a single one of his patients in the second half of their lives whose problem could not have been solved by contact with the "numinous" or the Absolute Center (Letters, vol. 1, 1973, p. 377). An extraordinary statement from a man who considered himself alienated from institutional religion! Yet thirty years later we find ourselves condemned to live in a world in which "the best lack all conviction and the worst are full of passionate intensity." The Center has not held. Most of the gods we have met in our narcissistic age have been no more than projected and magnified images of ourselves. The Catholic God looks Roman, the charismatic God looks sweet, the liberal God looks undemanding, and the American God looks tribal and pathetic.

We wait for the Word of the Lord. We wait for the season of the Word of the Lord. The falcon must hear the falconer.

Beginning with Death

MARY VINEYARD

Let in the wind,
Let in the rain,
Let in the moors tonight,

The storm beats at my window-pane,
Night stands at my bed-foot,
Let in the fear,
Let in the pain,
Let in the trees that toss and groan,
Let in the north tonight,

Let in the nameless formless power
That beats upon my door,
Let in the ice, let in the snow,
The banshees howling on the moor,
The bracken-bush on the bleak hillside,
Let in the dead tonight.
                        Kathleen Raine, *Northumbrian Sequence IV*

*I*n Celtic tradition, November 1 is the beginning of the new year. The wheel of time has circled once more and we are returned to our starting point. And this starting point, this new beginning, takes place not in bright rejoicing but in darkness. The sun is still waiting. This is the time of shadow, the Crone, the dead.

The past several thousand years of Western history have consisted of a concentrated panicked flight from darkness. And yet we know that life does begin in darkness; the seed buried in the earth, the child as single blind cell in the fluid interior of a woman. We know that what is new, young, small, and fragile must be hidden, contained, and kept away from the harsh flare of ambitious solar consciousness.

The darkness is shelter, a place of incubation, but it is also a place of fear. Each of us has heard the banshees howling on the moor, has seen night standing at the bed-foot. We have known the terror of meeting what we cannot understand, cannot control, cannot banish. And this too, is a good place to begin. For it is when we are cornered, overcome, and powerless, when all pretense of dominance, all inflation has disappeared, that we are ready to ask the real questions and to listen to answers that come from the voice of the wild wind.

We would like to flee from that voice, from the untamed, the "nameless formless power." But we do so at our peril. For that wildness is part of us, and even more importantly, it is part of God. God is the Ultimate, Untamable, the Uncontrollable, the Indefinable, Unnameable, Unspeakable. We have tried to whitewash God (literally, making "him" into a bearded white male), but the paint won't stick. Again and again divinity emerges in unexpected places, in surprising, even shocking forms. As Coyote, Kokopelli, Kali, Hekate, goat-footed, laughing, hurling thunderbolts, or healing lepers in Galilee. It's a cosmic hall of mirrors, and every face of God we see is also our own selves journeying through this life.

And this God also bears the face of death—which is why we must "let in the dead tonight." Life is, by definition, tragic. Life without death does not exist at all. If there are beginnings, there are also, necessarily, endings. If life is going anywhere at all, it is going inexorably toward death. Perhaps we have feared death because we have misunderstood it, have lost our memory of the ocean into which every river runs.

Let in the dead tonight, let in all your fears. Let in your weakness and all the things you cannot change. Let go, tonight, of everything you're holding on to, of everything that keeps you from beginning again. Let go of anything that tells you not to trust, that says God is not big enough to catch you anywhere you might leap. God is on the moors, is howling like a banshee, is coming for you, is standing at your bed-foot. God is all your history, your desires, your hopes.

The poem ends like this:

> Let in the wound,
> Let in the pain,
> Let in your child tonight.

Education and Soul-Making: Are We Killing or Nourishing the Spirit?

MIKE ROCHE

A dear friend recently asked me to moderate a panel on the general topic of "Spirituality, Commitment, and Work." About the same time, I happened across a review of a book entitled *Killing the Spirit—Higher Education in America*. The intersection of these two events set me to reflecting on the extent to which the work I have undertaken over the past sixteen years as a university professor has nourished or retarded the spiritual development of my students and myself. This inquiry demanded that I be clear and honest about the meaning of spirituality, about what education is and what it could be, and about how open I have been to reducing the distance between the present and the possible.

I am drawn to Alan Jones's characterization of spirituality as the "art of making connections" and I generally add "but not attachments." In other words, the more spiritual we are, the more artful we become at making connections with the divine, with each other, and with our Mother Earth—connecting not attaching, celebrating not clinging, reverencing not exploiting. This association between spirituality and reverence cannot be overstated. Thomas Berry's declaration, "Reverence will be total, or it will not be at all," corresponds well with the maxim, "We either contemplate or we exploit." Jones elaborates: "We either see things and persons with reverence and awe . . . or we appropriate them, and manipulate them for our own purposes." The more we open ourselves to possession by this holy reverence, the more we experience the divine blood that flows between us and unifies all that is.

Now I wish to explore whether the environment of contemporary higher education is congenial to the development of the sort of spirituality I have described. How much exposure to reverence and the art of making connections does the standard experience in higher education provide? I am not encouraged by what I see and feel. The renowned Brazilian educator Paulo Freire has used the term "culture of silence" to describe the unhealthy dimensions of the present system of education:

> One element is the students' internalizing passive roles scripted for them in the traditional classroom. The official pedagogy constructs them as passive/aggressive characters. After years in dull transfer-of-knowledge classes, in boring courses filled with sedating teacher-talk, many have become non-participants, waiting for the teacher to set the rules and start narrating what to memorize. These students are silent because they no longer expect education to include joy of learning, moments of passion or inspiration or comedy, or even that education will speak to the real conditions of their lives. They expect the droning voice of the teacher to fill the very long class hour. (A Pedogogy for Liberation, p. 122)

No wonder so many students drop out of education in all kinds of ways. The contemporary educational experience teaches much more about judgementalism and separation than about reverence and unity. Students are separated from their professors by the evaluative power the professors hold over them, by the almighty research the professors are "encouraged" to conduct even if it is to the detriment of their teaching, often by a lecture method of teaching that involves professors speaking only to and not with their students, and by the supposedly value-neutral and comprehensive professional expertise of the professor. Students are separated from one another by a competitive environment that grants only a limited number of "good" grades and ultimately good jobs, by a fear of failure that is heightened under these conditions, and by courses structured in such a fashion that students can easily go through the entire semester without saying a word to the persons sitting on either side of them. Students are also separated from the broader community: they learn for themselves and not for us at all, to satisfy their material desires rather than to put their knowledge to the service of the world. They are separated from ideas and from their own stories. Ideas and course content seem distant and uninteresting because there is so little effort to connect them with the concrete realities of the students' lives. Furthermore, since the contents of their lives are so rarely invited into the rigid agenda for the semester, students easily come to believe that their own stories and feelings are not only irrelevant but also unworthy. Finally, students are separated from the gloriously evolutionary and mysterious nature of life and learning. Contemporary education operates as though we can precisely objectify and control all that is and concentrates almost exclusively on mastering existing knowledge. Creating knowledge and traveling together with reverence into the Holy Unknown are aspirations that appear too lofty for the "higher" education of today.

It is clear to me now that most of what we do in higher education crushes rather than nourishes the Spirit that resides within us all. We are committing a great sin, allowing a great institutional evil to be perpetrated—and, in spite of all our learning, we can't name the unconscious conspiracy to silence the Spirit in which we are engaged. I am both saddened and maddened by this predicament because I sense the unique nature of the opportunities we are squandering and I cherish the tradition we are dishonoring. Erich Fromm wrote that when we merely convey knowledge, we are losing that teaching which is the most essential for human development: "The teaching which can only be given by the simple presence of a mature, loving person." Fromm reminds us that in previous epochs of our own and other cultures, the teacher was not solely or even primarily a source of information; rather, his or her function was to pass along certain human attitudes. "This tradition is not primarily based on the transmission of certain kinds of knowledge, but of certain kinds of human traits. If the coming generations will not see these traits anymore, a five-thousand-year-old culture will break down, even if knowledge is transmitted and further developed." So teaching can be a way of soul-making. It, along with farming and healing can be one of the three great cooperative arts. Through the mirror of relationship, teachers and students can often stop the world and their lives long enough to examine them for unhealthy and unjust patterns. Through this same mirror, students and teachers can discover their greatest gifts, accept them as such, and detect the places of suffering and injustice in the world to which those gifts are intended to flow. Alan Jones contends that soul-making "is a matter of choosing a certain paradigm or model. And the choice makes all the difference." Education in this tradition offers students and teachers a model of existence—of who we are and what our lives should be about—that is much more comprehensive, connected, inspiring, and graceful than the constricted contemporary vision to which we are so accustomed and perhaps even addicted.

The process of letting go of this addiction has been very difficult for me. I am learning the hard but only way about how important control, knowledge, and power are to me. I am also learning about how desperately my ego sometimes feeds on the role of "star" professor and how little encouragement this environment gives me to do otherwise. I view myself as a recovering "star" professor. My recovery has been nurtured by a holy host of events and influences. Without going into any detail, I can identify experiences in our family life, in my prison work, in traveling and working in developing countries, and in the internship I completed at the CAC that have been essential junctures on my road to recovery. Mid-life has also had something to do with it. Robert Bly believes that in their forties and fifties, most men particularly go through a process of either embedding themselves further into the life and ideologies of the institutions with which they are involved or of severing their links with those institutions in more or less radical ways. I'm doing much more severing than embedding these days. I don't want to be one of those academics Bly describes who resemble gray jars: "people totally unable to merge into the place where they live—they could live in a valley for years and never become the valley." Bly cites Antonio Machado, who elaborates further on gray jar academics:

> Everywhere I've gone I've seen
> excursions of sadness
> angry and melancholy
> drunkards with black shadows,
>
> And academics in offstage clothes
> who watch, say nothing, and think
> they know, because they do not
> drink wine in the ordinary bars.

One final, and perhaps the most powerful, influence has come to my aid in confronting the gray-jar addictions that bind me. The students I have learned with over the past sixteen years are the ones I need to credit most for showing me the way off the beaten path. This may seem unlikely in light of all the impediments to student spirituality I have discussed, and I am certainly not suggesting that all students are in the same place in this regard. I do know, however, that every time my soul has become so sore that I felt I had either to try something more spiritually nourishing in my teaching or to quit, there have always been students who have stepped forward to support me and challenge me to open further to the Spirit. Student souls are also sore. In fact, I believe that there are many students who are literally dying for spiritual nourishment. We don't provide it in the educational environment and they don't get it elsewhere, so they turn desperately to cults, drugs, alcohol, money, status, work, and more in order to medicate the pain they often cannot name.

The most recent instance in which the students and I have collaborated in opening to the Spirit involves a course I have offered for the past several years entitled Justice and Compassion. For me, the experience has served as a holy oasis in an otherwise desolate spiritual desert. The group is small: twelve to fifteen of us, self-selected after a conversation I have with each prospective member describing the untraditional nature of the course. The content of the course is not typical for a university curriculum. The past term we read *How Can I Help?* by Ram Dass and Paul Gorman, *Justice: The Restorative Vision* by Daniel Van Ness et al., *The Seed and the Tree—A Reflection on Nonviolence* by Daniel Seeger, *An Interrupted Life* by Etty Hillesum, and *On Education* by J. Krishnamurti. But it is not so much the contents as it is the process of this experience that truly sets it apart. We sit in a circle and we begin each session with a meditation offered voluntarily by one of our members. The meditation is followed by a reflective period of silence and a "breaking of bread" together (anything from pizza to ice cream and cookies) that comes from a picnic basket that circulates among us throughout the semester. As we move into a discussion of the readings for the day, we very intentionally relate them to our own stories. I believe, with Mary Rose O'Reilley, that "when people tell their stories, everything changes . . . Standing firmly in your story gives you identity and voice; it keeps you from being regimented, objectified, and turned into a thing." So we tell our stories and we allow them to interact with theory and analytical frameworks. Freire would say that through this process we become more adept at reading the word and the world. Both our theories and our stories become more relevant and authentic.

At some point during the semester, when we all agree the timing is right, we move beyond the walls of our classroom in some sort of service capacity. We determine when and where we will serve strictly by consensus and we share the responsibility of contacting the various agencies and institutions where we might work. Our service outings generally occur outside the regularly scheduled class time; we all serve together and we do not schedule a function unless all of us can attend. This process of coordinating our busy schedules has itself proven to be an invaluable exercise in community building, empowerment, and exploring alternatives to the violent ways we often treat each other. This past term we ventured reverently out seven times to work in prison, mental health facilities, shelters for the homeless, and in a transition house. I do not have the capacity to convey in written word the impact of these experiences on us all. Gibran said, "Work is love made visible." Through our work, we enter into the lives and stories of others with whom we are not often used to spending time and who may look at the world in ways quite different from our own. We spend time "drinking wine in ordinary bars." We see the world as so many do—from the bottom up—and we comprehend more about the unjust conditions that keep people down. These experiences enrich our stories, reveal our relationships with each other, and generally compel a further expansion of our theories, paradigms, and models of existence. One student wrote in his reflective journal:

> I had always heard of love described as a creative force but shrugged it off as figurative drivel. Not to say I didn't believe in love, of course I did—romantic love, family love, even brotherly love . . . but love as a means of social change? A vehicle for justice in the human condition? Don't be absurd. This is reserved for economic manipulation, political action, social revolution; force, force, force . . .
>
> But , . . . "I once was lost but now I am found, I was blind and now I see." What a fool I had been. What have we profited through the materialistic interpretation? Alienated ourselves from our inner world, from each other, disintegrated our families, waged war with our brothers and sisters, enslaved the mi-

norities and those who labor, aborted our unborn, raped our women, ravaged our environment, stockpiled arms, and brought the planetary ecology to the brink of annihilation. We have gained the world—but lost every soul including our own.

Now it is all so clear. We are all in this together—human, bird, dolphin, tree, mountain, cloud, sky, sea, earth. The salvation and liberation of one is wrapped up in that of everything else. Everything is in us, and we are everything. To see that is the fear of God—it is the beginning of Wisdom.

At the end of the semester, we gathered at my farmhouse for a closing ceremony. There was much laughter, gift-giving, tearful statements of gratitude, and a holy covenant between us to keep this page in our lives alive. As we stood outside, arm-in-arm in our circle, singing a ritual song to seal our covenant, a giant full moon awoke slowly on the horizon. In its fullness we saw ourselves completely—no part left out—all together. At that precise and glorious moment we understood Shug in *The Color Purple:* "One day when I was sitting quiet and feeling like a motherless child, which I was, it came to me: that feeling of being a part of everything, not separate at all. I knew that if I cut a tree, my arm would bleed. And I laughed and I cried and I run all around the house." That's the kind of learning that helps make a soul.

Masculine Spirituality

RICHARD ROHR, OFM

*P*erhaps the term sounds new, different, even wrong or unnecessary. Why would we bother speaking of spirituality that is especially masculine or male? Is there anything to be learned here? Anything that can help both men and women to meet the Christ? I am convinced that there is. Let's see if we can look at it.

First of all, I want to say that a masculine spirituality is not just for men, although it is men who are most likely going to have to rediscover and exemplify it. Strangely, it is an approach that many women are more in touch with today than men. Women have been encouraged and even forced to do their inner work more than men in our culture. In general they are far ahead of men in integrating the masculine and feminine parts of themselves. Their inner journeys have left many of us guys in the dust. Our sisters' pursuit of the authentic feminine has made the brothers aware that there is also an authentic masculine. But what is it?

Quite simply, it is the other side of the feminine energy. It is the other pole, the contrary, the balance, the *yang* that is always the necessary complement to *yin* in Chinese harmony. For the Judaeo-Christian tradition it is half of the image of God: "God created humanity as a self-image, male and female God created them" (Gen. 1:27). I am *not* saying that males are characterized by exclusively masculine energy and women only by feminine. Quite the contrary, although there has been a tendency in most cultures to stereotype, classify, and hold the sexes in one predictable type of energy and behavior. Unfortunately, I believe this has kept us immature, unwhole, compulsive and unready for true love-making—human or divine.

St. Paul says, "There can be neither male nor female, for you are all one in Christ Jesus" (Gal. 3:28). The new humanity that we are pointed toward is not neuter or unisex or oversexed, all of which make love impossible. In Christ we are whole, one, in union, integrated, the self, wholly holy. That is the final product of the Spirit making all things one. It is the consummate achievement of God in Christ who reconciles all things within himself (Col. 1:20) and invites us into the ongoing reconciliation of all things (Eph. 5:18). As a celibate male religious I can make little sense of my state unless I find some way to awaken and love my own inner feminine soul. Without it, I am merely a self-centered bachelor, a would-be creator, a dried up root.

A man without his feminine soul is easily described. His personality will move toward the outer superficial world and his head will be his control tower. He will build, explain, use, fix, manipulate, legislate, order, and play with whatever he bothers to touch, but will not really touch it at all. For he does not know the inside of things. In fact, he is afraid of it, and that is why the control tower of reason and pseudocontrol works overtime. It is the only way to give himself a sense of security and significance. He is trapped in part of the picture, which is dangerous precisely because he thinks it is the whole picture. He is trapped inside the false masculine. Corporately, these have become the myths of Western civilization. They are largely written by men who have controlled the power, the money, the corporations, the church, the military, the morality books. What we call "reality" and are almost totally addicted to is largely a construct of men who frankly have not done their inner work. They have not gone inside, they have not learned trust, vulnerability, prayer, or poetry. They and the civilization we have inherited from them are in great part unwhole or even sick, while calling themselves sane. Until males and cooperating females recognize this unwholeness, this anti-Christianity posing as the real thing, we have no hope of making love to the full Christ. We will, in fact, be threatened by his wholeness and substitute (as we generally have) little schemes for salvation for daring religious faith. Basically we transfer the business world of win/ achieve/prove/success/control/ to the realm of the Spirit. And it just doesn't work. God knows, we have tried for enough centuries! Quality testing of nation and church tells me there must be a better way. It's called conversion.

Conversion to the no-me. Conversion to the other, the alien, the would-be enemy that we must learn to love. Men must be converted to the feminine and women to the masculine. Maybe that is why God made sexual attraction so compelling. If we are converted to the nonself, everything changes. In that it approaches authentic religious conversion (the utter not-me: God) more than any other type of conversion. From the whole—and Center—position, we see through eyes other than our own half-blinded ones. We see the other side of things and forgiveness becomes possible. We see that the enemy is not enemy but spiritual helpmate. There is nothing more to defend and nothing more to be afraid of once we have met and accepted our inner opposite. Not all opposites offer us possibility and transcendence.

A masculine spirituality would emphasize action over theory, service to the human community over religious discussions, truth-speaking over social graces, and doing justice over looking nice. Without a complementary masculine, spirituality becomes overly feminine (which is really false feminine!) and is characterized by too much inwardness, too much preoccupation with relationship, a morass of unclarified feelings, and endless selfprotectiveness. In my humble masculine opinion, I believe that much of the modern, sophisticated church is swirling in this false feminine. It is one of the main reasons that doers, movers, shakers, and change agents have largely given up on church people and church groups. As one very effective woman said to me recently, "After a while you get tired of all the in-house jargon that seems to go nowhere." A false feminine spirituality is the trap of those with lots of leisure, luxury, and liberal ideas. They have the option *not* to do. Their very liberalism becomes an inoculation against the whole and radical Gospel.

A masculine spirituality would be one that encourages men to take that radical Gospel journey from their unique beginning point, in their own unique style, with their own unique goals—without doubt or apology or imitation of their sisters (or mothers, for that matter). That of itself takes immense courage and self-possession. A man with such a spirituality has life for others and knows it. He does not need to push, intimidate, or play the power games common to other men, because he possesses his power with surety and calm self-confidence. He is not opinionated or arrogant, but he knows. He is not needy or bothered by status symbols, because he is. He does not need monogrammed briefcases and underwear, his identity is settled and secure—and within. He possesses his soul and does not give it lightly to corporations, armies, nation-states, and the acceptable collective thinking.

Saints trust their masculine soul because they have met the Father. He (sic!) taught them about anger, passion, power, and clarity. He told them to go all the way through and pay the price for it (don't send the bill to others). He shared with them his own creative seed, his own decisive Word, his own illuminating Spirit. They are comfortable knowing and they are comfortable not knowing. They can care and not care without guilt. They can act without success because they have named their fear of failure. They do not need to affirm or deny, judge or ignore. But they are free to do all of them with impunity. The saints are invincible. They are men!

A masculine spirituality has taken a long time to emerge in a healthy way for many reasons, I'm sure. The state needed conformists and unfeeling warriors to go about its business, and "holy Mother Church" seemed to want children more than bridegrooms. But I am convinced that the most fundamental reason why men and women have failed to love and trust their masculine energy is the overriding "Father Wound" that is carried by the vast majority of people in Western civilization. Those have a Father Wound who have never been touched by their human father. Either he had no time, no freedom, or no need, but the end result is children who have no masculine energy. They will lack self-confidence and the ability to do, carry through, and trust themselves—because they were never trusted by him.

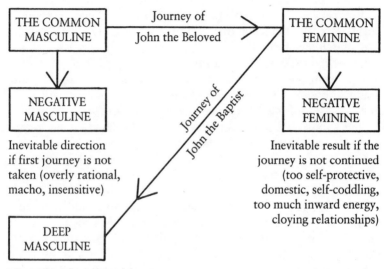

The Holy Man or "Wild Man"

If there is one very good reason for God to reveal himself as the *Father* of Jesus, it is because that is where most people are unfeeling, unbelieving, and unwhole. With Philip the apostle, we all join in: "Lord, show us the Father, and we shall be satisfied" (John 14:8). Without the facing, feeling, and restoring of this wound, I am sure that most people will continue to live lives of pseudomasculinity: business and bravado as usual, dishonest power instead of honest powerlessness. And the sons and daughters of the next generation will repeat the sad process—unfathered.

Is there a way out? There is. But only for "men." There is no way to masculinity. Masculinity is the way. Name the wound. Feel and weep over the wound. (That is strength, not weakness.) Seek the face of the Father. (That is action and journey, not passivity.) Own and take full responsibility for your life and behavior. Don't blame, sit in shame, or wait for warm feelings and miracles. Act as if. Do it. Go with it. Risk it.

Call it phallic faith if you will, but do not doubt the seed within you. I have always felt that was the unconscious but real motive for circumcision in the Jewish religion: It is going to hurt to be a man, to give life, to create. There is a price for being of the covenant—and you had better be reminded of that right at the beginning and right at the point. (Yep, I said it!)

Masculine faith does not doubt the seed within. But God's sons are without dignity, self-confidence or true power. We look like the oppressors, dear sisters, but have no doubt we are really the oppressed. We believe the false promises of the system even more than you, and now we are trapped at what is supposed to be the top. We need you, we need our feminine souls, we need fathers and brothers, we need an also masculine God to find our way back into the human circle. We need ourselves—from the inside.

The unique character of this male journey is that we must make it like no other journey: alone, apart, trusting that deepest Self which is silent, unyielding, but utterly alive. By definition, there can be no maps, no certitudes, no shortcuts. It can't just be talked through, imitated, or role-played. The male journey must be *done*—by me.

Wrestling with Personal Demons on the Road to Nonviolence

LINDA HARDY

I've heard it said that authentic peacemaking is one of the most direct routes to conversion because you can't fake it for very long— you eventually run headlong into the violence of your own heart. My own experience in raising children has born that out and has made the issue of nonviolence a personal one for me—not primarily a way of saving the world, at this point, but a way of saving my children from the darkness within myself. The only way to save them from it, I have found, is for me to travel more deeply into it myself.

The violence I'm talking about is not physical, but is violence nonetheless—a kind of mean-spiritedness that comes out under pressure and gets directed at my oldest child, a five-year-old boy. I am not talking about simply losing my temper now and then, but of unleashing on him a rage of demons that has more to do with me than with any behavior of his. At moments like these, I hear myself speaking in a voice that shocks me, frightens my children, and leaves me wondering, "Where did that come from?"

The irony in all this is that when I was growing up as the youngest of three children, my father used to call me the peacemaker of the family. If he were alive today I'd ask him what he meant by that, because I don't remember actively intervening to keep the peace. If I tried, I certainly didn't succeed, because there were many nights when everybody seemed to be yelling at everybody else, and I was spared, I guess, only because I didn't antagonize anybody or take sides. For many years afterwards I thought that the fury of the storms that swirled around me as a child did not affect me as an adult, that somehow I had escaped unharmed, like someone traveling in the eye of the hurricane. It was only later, as a parent, when I heard the fury in my own voice, that I realized how much of the storm I still carry within me.

The fury erupts, now and then, in a lightning bolt of blistering words, burning my son and setting off a firestorm in me. The fire burns away any illusion of my own goodness and sears into consciousness my own capacity for evil, an evil that is all of a piece with the kind that makes the evening news. With that knowledge, the evil of dictators, terrorists, and common criminals loses some of its otherness, because it starts to look like something I have seen in my own soul. I look at those people now and think, "That's the part of me that doesn't show."

It doesn't show because I was "properly socialized," first by the love of my parents and then by social institutions that served me well. There was no reason for me to be devious or belligerent when I could get whatever I wanted just by being nice. But the evil that I could do, within my own small sphere of influence, is the evil I have done.

It came to me as follows during one of my bouts of demon-wrestling: I saw myself looking in the windows of a tall apartment building and seeing in each room a typical middle-class North American family, well-dressed and well-fed. But what I was also aware of in these scenes—not intellectually, but viscerally—was the intensity of neurotic misery that lay just below the surface. What made the image one of almost crushing sorrow for me was the realization that I was sowing the seeds of that kind of suffering in my own son.

But if this insight had turned into a funeral pyre of guilt, I would not be writing about it as a conversion experience. What made it a conversion was the realization that when I stopped defending against the evil in my own heart and acknowledged my oneness with the other evildoers of the world, that was the point at which I became one with Christ, who, as Paul said, "became sin" for our sake. I joined him on the cross and allowed my darkness to merge with his; the fire of self-knowledge that first lit up and then destroyed every illusion had finally gone out, leaving me in total darkness.

I woke up the next morning feeling like someone in a burned-out house. There was space and light all around where there used to be roof and walls, and that gave me a good view of the landscape. I saw dry riverbeds where I always thought there was plenty of water, and that explained why one son rather than the other bore the brunt of my anger—he was the one most likely to ask for water when I was down to stones, and for drawing attention to that barrenness he also drew my wrath. Knowing that, I could at least locate the problem within myself instead of projecting it onto him, and thus fight my own demons on my own turf. So even if I could not give him what I'd like, I reasoned, I could still give him the benefit of this self-knowledge and so bless with ashes what I couldn't bless with water.

But something in me rebelled at making this wounded wisdom, valid as it is, the last word. Deep down, I still believe life is about joy. I've always believed that, but in the past, joy to me meant enjoyment—of beauty, of other people, of my own capacity for happiness. All of these things are as delightful as springs bubbling up out of rock, but liable to be lost in a dry season, as I've discovered. It is the deep underground source that draws me now, but I know that I have to move deeper into my own darkness before I can claim it. For that reason, it was a fortunate fire that destroyed my house, because on the site of its ruined foundations my journey inward began in earnest—a journey into my own depths, past my own demons, to the common ground of being, where just being is joy itself.

So far, I have described this as an intensely personal journey. But the social implications of it became clear to me over the summer when events of personal and political significance coincided.

The day after I woke up in a burned-out house, my son asked me to help him make a sword and shield. I'm normally not very good at that kind of thing, but that afternoon I was able to become wholly absorbed in the project and make a sword and shield that we were both proud of. The sword was made of three layers of cardboard stapled together and then wrapped in clear tape, at his request, so it would "shine in the sun."

For a coat of arms on his shield he wanted the American flag, and for a motto, "God is for the U.S.A." (I resisted the impulse to comment on that, because I knew he meant, "God is for *me*.")

Then he wanted to test the strength of his shield by having me throw rocks at it. At first I balked, but then I saw the beauty of it—that this was a way of testing not only the strength of his shield but also the strength of his own small person against whatever meanness I could hurl at it. Since I could not call back the demons I had unleashed on him, I thought, I could at least give him the symbolic experience of fending them off.

So we stood outside in the patch of dirt by our back door and I started throwing against his shield some pebbles that he took obvious delight in deflecting, his blond, wiry frame jumping around in the gathering darkness like a dancing lightning bolt in a dark cloud.

Reflecting on the fact that it had been his lot in life, by temperament or by birth order, to "draw the lightning" of my own repressed rage, I realized that by drawing it to himself, he also drew it out of me, like venom out of a snakebite. And by doing so, he also took a small amount of violence out of the public domain, lowering a bit the reservoir of pent-up aggression that fuels so much of public life, from the Rambo energy at one end of the spectrum to the self-righteous rhetoric of the peace movement at the other end. In both cases, it seems to me, there is an "us against them" mentality rooted in fear and hatred of the "other"—a denial of the "other" within.

This connection between the personal and the public reality was brought home to me when I opened the paper a few days later and saw that an American hostage had been killed in the Middle East and the President was considering bombing raids against the Muslim extremists thought to be responsible for it.

Now the idea of a military raid to avenge someone's death or protect the honor of the United States has never had much hold on me. On the other hand, after the deed was done, the death of terrorists, like the execution of a mass murderer, usually found me of two minds and therefore of two voices: "Of course I don't condone that kind of thing," my upstairs voice would say. "But I'm glad they got what they deserved," a voice from the cellar would answer.

This time, perhaps because the lightning and venom had just been drawn out of me, I heard myself speaking with one voice instead of two, and that voice had forgotten the retaliatory instinct completely enough, at least for the moment, to be genuinely mystified: "Now why in the world would they do a thing like that?"

I had discovered, in other words, that the roots of authentic nonviolence are not in the upper reaches of highmindedness but in the lower depths of personal darkness, where the "oneness of humanity" is not an idealistic slogan but an experienced reality.

But it is not the darkness itself that makes for conversion. Often as not it makes for revulsion—a rejection of the wormy underground of our common humanity and the building of a house of illusion over it. In that case, the darkness becomes not the fertile soil of conversion but the hidden ground of despair.

For me, it was meeting Christ in this darkness that made it otherwise. That is what allowed me to lose my own house and yet feel no desire to rebuild it. It was a loss I counted as gain.

Confessions of A
New Age Junkie

REBECCA WOOD

*F*resh from the shower, Raymond returns to the service center and asks to use deodorant. He unbuttons his shirt and publicly—we're in a shelter for the homeless—completes his ablutions. Although he's reticent and it's our first meeting, his pride in a new shepherding job slips out. That I know a little "pastor" lingo and am a spinner of fleece supports our exchange. We share delight in a good lambing season with no lambs lost. His small flock of two dozen belongs to a Navajo relative and pastures in the Jemez Mountains northwest of Albuqueruqe. Raymond had managed a day off to return to St. Martin's Day Shelter and extend the storage of his possessions.

That evening, I create a dinner of my choice in a home of my choice where I enjoy private ablutions. My meal fills my belly and what fills me more deeply is the epiphany of those few minutes with Raymond. Today I'd extended countless towels, razors, and portions of shampoo. In one exchange—ostensibly about sheep, fleece, and toiletries—there was a meeting. A shared moment. An exchange of realities. A spaciousness that allowed us to be present to each other. The gift of such a movement is transformation.

This richness that I often taste at St. Martin's stands in stark contrast to the "rich" life of experiences that I come from. Yes, I was a New Age junkie in hot pursuit of transforming experiences.

Fresh out of college, the 1960s plucked me from my sheltered Utah existence and plopped me into Haight Ashbury. However, despite its misdirection, two themes from that era continue to serve me well: a rejection of the status quo and the embrace of holism. It was the latter, this hunger for integration of body, mind, and spirit, that soon propelled me from the Haight full tilt into Eastern health and religious studies. For twenty years I bounced between gurus and trends. Throughout this time I lived in various alternative communities, and, as a journalist, my assignments took me from Stonehenge to Machu Picchu. I covered untold conferences and meetings with New Age figureheads and spiritual contenders. And while some experiences supported my inner growth, much of it did not. My lifeline out was my conversion to Catholicism five years ago, a deepening meditation practice, and spiritual direction from a skilled advisor.

The part of the New Age movement that makes me cringe is its perpetration of dilettantism and power. Nuggets from this tradition and nuggets from that provided me with a comfortable hodgepodge of values and enabled me to bypass accountability. Among many New Agers, dilettantism is the modus operandi. What's more disturbing, however, is the quest for psychic power. While shamanism is the current buzz word for this power, magic is its less fashionable tag. Much of the New Age spirituality is about garnering such power. It is assured that this will be used for the good. But remember, accountability is not this movement's strength. In my observation, a power-wielding person not accountable to a vital community is best avoided.

I recently read a useful Zen Buddhist description of the levels of power. Yasutani Roshi observed that some religions place great importance upon *makyo* or "mysterious vision." Be it visions, channeling, speaking in tongues, astral traveling, levitation, or psychic surgery, these phenomena tend to be mistaken as signs of enlightenment and salvation. Yasutani Roshi said, "These phenomena may be of general interest, for they reveal the rich potential of human experience, but they reveal little of the true nature of the one who experiences them. . . ." In Zen, *makyo* are a sign that you are making progress with your practice, but the Roshi advises us to "let them go as you would any other delusion."

The examples of both Buddha and Jesus are illustrative. At the end of a period of extreme asceticism, the Buddha sat under the Bodhi tree and was tempted by *makyo* of beautiful women, angels, and devils. Likewise the devil tempted Jesus at the end of his desert fast. For both Buddha and Jesus, renunciation of delusion triggered enlightenment and the beginning of public ministry.

I recall the times I've oohed and aahed at *makyo*—a medicine man evoking an eagle in a sweat lodge, a Philippine psychic surgeon removing gunk from my gut. What a relief no longer to be a groupie. I am not criticizing traditional peoples or their belief systems; rather, I criticize myself and my New Age cronies for lusting after and tallying up experiences and/or displays of supernatural power just as materialists lust after and tally up tangible symbols of power.

Today, Raymond—from a position of utter powerlessness—asks to use deodorant. His vulnerability presents an opportunity: an opportunity for me to shed my inflated self-importance. Rampant want stands poignant contrast to the smallness of what I have to give. But I give. In so doing. I am filled.

A Virus of Kindness

AVIS CROWE

"*P*ractice random kindness and senseless acts of beauty." The words leapt out from the array of announcements about aerobics classes and special fitness programs. Normally I walk right by the bulletin board on my way to swim, but this particular morning the unexpected words scrawled on a little white card grabbed my attention.

I felt both recognition and kinship: recognition of a practice as old as time—spontaneous acts of generosity, care, and foolishness that some people have quietly engaged in forever. I think of two women friends of the CAC who are constitutionally unable *not* to engage in such acts! Who but Beth and Shirley would drive to where the staff was on the downside of a two-day planning retreat, bearing armloads of purple balloons and a card with loving nonsense that wished us well in our deliberations! I felt a personal kinship with the author of those words, for with them she legitimized something I have attempted now and again on a small scale, sometimes feeling vaguely silly and even mildly guilty when I'm "caught!" I renewed my own commitment to such foolishness as I tucked the provocative words in my heart, pondering them as I went about my day.

Some weeks later, a friend wrote me a brief note and enclosed a 1991 editorial from *Glamour* magazine. The title? "Practice Random Kindness and Senseless Acts of Beauty." The writer characterizes it as "an underground slogan that's spreading across the nation." It is evidently appearing on car bumpers and refrigerator doors as well as swim-club bulletin boards. One woman who saw it painted on a warehouse wall copied it down and now includes it as a kind of footnote to every letter she writes.

I understand the impulse; I copied the article and sent it to a number of friends. To see the words is to become an evangelist, spreading the word, preaching the good news! To hear the stories of how others have acted on them is to want to jump into the game too. The words beg us to lighten up, to reach out and help, to do a favor for someone without their knowing it, without hanging around to be acknowledged or thanked.

This kind of spontaneous good-heartedness is catching. To be on the receiving end of the unexpected gesture is to be "surprised by joy," to borrow a phrase from C. S. Lewis (who borrowed it from Wordsworth) and to want to pass it on. Have you ever been caught short of change and had a stranger give what you needed? I have, and it set me up for the whole day, prompting me to do the same later on. It's even more fun to set the chain in motion. At the bakery for the ritual morning coffee and muffin following a recent swim, I spilled some milk and went to get a damp cloth. As I was about to take it back to the counter, I saw the messy tables. No longer occupied, they were cluttered with empty paper cups and plates, crumpled napkins, crumbs, and bits of uneaten donuts. It had obviously been a busy morning, and the women behind the counter seemed frazzled. Without much thought, since the cloth was already in hand, I set about cleaning up, throwing out the trash, and wiping the tables. I returned the cloth, taking great delight in the astonished response and in the energy I felt surge through my body as I headed out the door.

I believe there is within each of us just such an impulse to kindness, to a crazy generosity that prompted one person after reading the slogan to pay for the next six cars as she went through a highway tollbooth! Yet many of us have become stingy with these impulses, afraid to demonstrate such "deviant" behavior. In this age of litigation, random violence, suspicion, and simple haste, it's easy to lose our spontaneity, our willingness to act a bit peculiar, to be a fool for God! One day at the supermarket check-out line, I was very aware that the young woman behind the counter was frustrated and angry, about at the end of her tether. I thought at the time how nice it would be to go get a few posies to give her. But I was in a hurry and let the impulse pass. I wish I hadn't.

"Practice random kindness and senseless acts of beauty." This innocent string of words encourages us to act on those basic instincts for kindness and the small gesture that can transform a grumpy day into one of spaciousness and light. We have clothed ourselves and one another in suspicion for too long. Now someone has thrown the door open wide, letting in light and fresh air, encouraging us to come out and play!

Although a friend of mine intensely dislikes the comparison, it's not unlike a virus, one that we should all do our best to catch and help spread until it becomes an epidemic and we are transformed into a nation of fools practicing random kindness and senseless acts of beauty.

Leaving the Woods

DYCKMAN W. VERMILYE

I left the woods for as good a reason as I went there. Perhaps it seemed to me that I had several more lives to live, and could not spare any more time for that one.
Henry David Thoreau, *Walden*

*N*early all of us are conditioned to believe that we have but one life to live. And many of us have been brought up to think that once we get a job, we'll stay in that job area for the rest of our lives. We are, after all, influenced by that medieval notion that a son would be what his father was. A man born a woodsman died a woodsman; a farmer's son became a farmer.

But we look less to fathers for vocational direction today, perhaps because fewer fathers are woodsman or farmers. I did not look to my father for vocational direction, nor did I follow in his footsteps. But it was expected that the one-vocation life would prevail for me, particularly if I chose to enter either a white-collar or a professional field. However, government statistics today show that men move from one vocation to another frequently during their working lives. The amount of time before a career change occurs rarely exceeds ten years. That's not a promotion within a field or a move from one position to comparable responsibilities for another employer; that's a complete career change.

"What do you want to be when you grow up?" remains a conversational opener for adults who don't know what else to say to a child, and the question implies that only one answer is expected. Pity the poor child who replies, "Well, I'm thinking of business for the first fifteen years, then some social service work, and I plan to spend the final years making furniture"!

I know something of the difficulty of deciding to live more than one life. When I was fifty-five, I decided that I could spare no more time for the professional field that had occupied my life and thoughts up to then. Most of my colleagues translated my decision to move on as one to "retire." There was no other way for many of them to deal with the possibility that I might want to leave one field and enter another completely different one. But I felt that I had climbed one ladder. I could see and feel the top rung and at times felt that I had a firm grip on it. The climb, I sensed, had been far more satisfying and stimulating than the time spent holding the top rungs of the ladder. Why not climb another one?

I was open by then to the notion that a man could work in more than one career field. I had come to value the concept that our society supports lifelong learning. Even though I had two graduate degrees, I realized that there was nothing to stop me from going back to school and being trained in another area if I wanted to do so. I had begun to counsel others to do that very thing. So it is not surprising that the moment came when I said to myself, "Put your life where your heart is. No more urging others. Do it yourself." I was no stranger to life-planning exercises and had worked myself through a series of values clarification exercises. But even so, there was much uncertainty about what another life would be. I realized that if I had to know what lay beyond the narrow gate of decision before I decided to go through, I would never go.

I went.

"Aren't you giving up your retirement program?" "Why leave when you have it already made?" "Isn't this a little—well—frivolous at your age?" These were the kinder reactions. I'm sure there were other comments that I never heard. I suspect now that the thought of a reasonably traditional and successful man purposefully looking for another life to lead was somehow disturbing and threatening to other reasonably traditional and successful men.

Inside, I had some of the same questions. It's funny now to realize how difficult it was at times to consider other specific jobs. When a chance to go into a business venture presented itself, my first thought was, "What will my academic colleagues think?" I had to spend some time working with that question until it resolved itself into, "Would I like to do that?" Not only our histories weigh us down; the price we pay for peer group membership is heavy.

The decision to go through the narrow gate was not made without considering the consequences to loved ones in my family. The freedom that living several lives meant to me was not synonymous with "doing my own thing." Had I grown up thirty or forty years later (and not gone straight from college into the Second World War, into marriage, and into graduate school), I might have done things differently. But the freedom to consider different ways of moving into manhood did not seem possible for me at the time. I am old enough now to appreciate how important it is for a father to encourage his son to look at many options when thinking about how he will live his life.

There is a story about Hassidic rabbis that I have enjoyed, even though it may be apocryphal. I have always understood that they were forbidden to study metaphysics until they were at least thirty years old. Younger than that, they were not considered sufficiently mature to appreciate the intricacies and subtleties of their subject. With the simple passage of time, metaphysics was presumed to be transformed for most learners from a philosophical study into a vivid mirror of life. Maybe we have had it backwards all along and should learn from this story. Maybe choices about how to live one's life should not be put to children until they are over thirty—or fifty-five!

I have no regrets about having decided on a new life at fifty-five and a different ladder to test out. Now, fifteen years after having made that first decision, I have had at least four identifiably different life experiences—including selling real estate in suburban Washington, D.C., four years in Africa, and now being on the staff at the Center. Who can tell how many more lives there are ahead?

Psychotherapy and Meditation

MARY VINYARD

*I*n May I attended a retreat in the Colorado Rocky Mountains on Psychotherapy and Meditation. The retreat was sponsored by the Buddhist Peace Fellowship and led by Thich Nhat Hanh and Sister Cao Phuong. Both are in exile from their home in Vietnam because of their nonpartisan relief work begun more than twenty years ago during the war. They now live in France in a community called Plum Village.

Thich Nhat Hanh (Thay) extols the wisdom and experience of the 2500-year-old Buddhist tradition, but he also believes that his teachings can be helpful to all people, both those who consider themselves Buddhist and those who do not.

The heart of Thay's teaching is mindfulness—simple awareness of the present moment and of what we are doing in it. Mindfulness makes us and the beings and objects around us real and really present. We miss a great deal of life by doing more than one thing at a time, or by doing one thing and thinking of another. So we live through many hours, many days without ever really being there at all.

The most powerful tool for entering mindfulness is breathing. Just breathing. Paying attention to the breath, knowing I am breathing, helps me to slow to a biologically natural pace, to stop thinking. Thinking is an excellent skill, but too often it is merely internal chatter, about the past or the future and not about the now. Thinking, Thay says, is less than being. Just breathing is being.

In addition to the rest and calm and the improved quality of life that mindfulness brings, its larger purpose is understanding. When I become aware and therefore present, when I am really here and my awareness has allowed the object of my awareness to be really here, I am able to see that object, to know and understand it. I touch its true nature because I know it experientially, not by thinking about it but by being with it.

One aspect of this true nature, this deep reality is what Thay calls interbeing. Nothing exists solely in and of itself, separate, independent, autonomous. When I see a flower, I see that it is created from and consists of non-flower elements. Sun and rain and earth and air and insects made the flower and are part of the flower still. When I see my Self, I see that I am also made of non-Self elements—pieces of my ancestors and my environment. My Self is real and the flower is real, but an isolated self and an independent flower are impossibilities, illusions.

Along with interbeing, another truth we understand through mindfulness is nonduality. Again, when I look at the flower, I see that it will soon decay. It will become compost, garbage. The garbage is already within it, part of it. And when I see the garbage, I know that it can decompose and become flowers. When everything is known as part of a cycle, as containing the seed of other forms, linear judgmental dualistic thinking stops.

Although the translation of these principles into therapeutic techniques is rich and fascinating territory, the most profound implications probably lie in the ways mindful living can create more health in ourselves. Many therapists agree that it is presence and relationship more than technique which facilitates healing. Therefore, whatever makes us more present and more related to our clients enhances our work. The practice of mindfulness will itself teach us much about understanding and compassion, about Self-seeing that is neither inflated nor deflated, about now-living that is neither anxious about the future nor remorseful about the past. All of these skills we can both live and share with our clients.

But the fruits of the practice are not just for ourselves and our clients. The Buddha's quest was for enlightenment, not for his own glorification but so that he could relieve the suffering of all beings. Practice, moment-by-moment commitment to mindfulness, leads to understanding, which leads to compassion, which leads to right action. We do not meditate to escape the world and the world's suffering but to become more and more engaged, more present to it. We begin to relieve suffering both by the actions to which our mindfulness leads us and by the mindfulness itself, by our increased ability to be peaceful and to enjoy happiness.

Thay and Sister Phuong encourage every psychotherapist to become also a peace activist. If we invest energy and care in supporting our clients in their healing process and yet do not try to improve the world in which this process has to take place, we are at the very least not making our own work any easier. How well can one become in a sick environment? How far can the healing process go in a world over which hangs the threat of nuclear destruction, or in which the air and food and water are poisoned, where species become extinct daily, where children are starving?

More importantly, engagement in relieving suffering is part of the healing process. We can neither heal nor be healed without being willing to give ourselves to the larger picture. Working for peace, justice, and planetary wellness is itself a meditation on interbeing, a way of planting and watering seeds of compassion and understanding, and lights a path for our clients to walk upon as well.

Perhaps the most paradoxical teaching is on the practice of smiling. It seems that life often and easily plants seeds of suffering and sadness in us and we learn the habit of noticing what is wrong. Thay believes we must practice awareness of what is not wrong. We need to cultivate the seeds of joy. What good will peace be to us if we have forgotten how to enjoy it? How much happiness do we miss because we do not know how to be happy about our happiness? And so the work, the meditation, the practice is not just sitting, but sitting and smiling, breathing and smiling, walking and smiling. I can learn not only to be in this present moment but to recognize it as and allow it to be the best moment of my life.

This practice teaches us to live without hope. We can stop waiting for things to get better. We can finally realize that this moment is the one that counts, the only one there is. Taking care of this moment is the only way to care for the past or the future. Hope, or a misunderstanding of hope, has so often been an excuse not to take action now, not to be happy now. Real hope is only about now, is present-based, is a simple firm confidence in the true nature of reality, in garbage becoming flowers.

In telling stories of their lives and work, Thay and Sister Phoung lovingly and dramatically illustrated the effectiveness of their teachings and practice. In Vietnam they taught their students to breathe and smile as they buried the dead. They learned to caress and hold and breathe through their anger as they helped rebuild bombed villages for the third and fourth time. Their understanding of interbeing taught them not to hate as friends and coworkers were killed. Now in exile they remain in contact with those still suffering at home and find ingenious ways to provide assistance. They also visit refugees around the world and invite refugee families to live for periods of time at Plum Village as a way of mending their shattered lives. They are even doing retreats for American Vietnam veterans who were also shattered by the war and are desperately in need of understanding, compassion, and forgiveness.

Many peace activists doing similar work sometimes suffer from burnout, from despair, and from temptations to hate. Thay and Sister Phuong speak eloquently of the way they have found to move through and beyond these struggles. What is obvious to them is that the practice is not about feeling but about being free of the feeling, being disidentified from it enough not to be overwhelmed, enough to choose and carry out whatever action the moment calls for. As they speak of their concern for suffering people it is obvious that feeling and caring are very much a part of their lives. But through practice and patience, feeling has become a tool and a source of energy rather than a stumbling block or a drain. They know how to let the garbage become flowers.

During the retreat, one participant told a story of a three-year-old boy who begged his parents to let him be alone with his newborn brother. Finally consenting, the parents listened from the next room as the child said to the baby, "quick, tell me where you came from! Tell me where you came from and tell me about God. I'm beginning to forget."

I am beginning to forget. Every day. So I ask babies and Buddhist teachers. I ask flowers and garbage. I ask Earth and Self and the moment. "Tell me where you came from. Tell me about God." This, I believe, is what psychotherapy and meditation, justice and peace work, breathing and smiling and being are about. They are about all of us, together, beginning to remember.

Prayer as a Political Activity

RICHARD ROHR, OFM

*J*esus went apart and prayed before he chose his committee of twelve. Francis says in his "Testament" that "no one told me what I should do, but the Most High himself made it clear . . . those who embrace this life must give everything to the poor . . . we refused to have anything more." Thomas Merton went off to a secluded monastery and his writings subverted Catholic America: "God is never shown by the Bible merely as a supplement of human power and intelligence, but as the very ground and reality of that power." Martin Luther King gathered his followers for hours of prayer before they went to the streets to endure the insults of the bigoted. Those who could not find their nonviolent soul could not march. And Gandhi set the sun on the English empire "not by power, not by an army, but by God's Spirit" (Zech. 4:6 against the kings of Israel). You would think we would know by now.

To pray is to build your own house. To pray is to discover that Someone else is within your house. To pray is to recognize that it is not your house at all. To keep praying is to have no house to protect because there is only One House. And that One House is everybody's Home. In other words, those who pray from the heart actually live in a very different and ultimately dangerous world. It is a world that makes the merely physical world seem anemic, illusory, and relative. The word "Real" takes on a new meaning and we find ourselves judging with utterly new scales, weights, and standards. Be careful of such house-builders, for their loyalties will lie in very different directions. They will be very different kinds of citizens and the state will not so easily depend on their salute. That is the politics of prayer. And that is probably why truly spiritual people are always a threat to politicians of any sort. They want our allegiance and we can no longer give it. Our house is too big.

In *The Republic* Plato said that "all societies are governed by the selfish interests of the ruling class." That was 380 years before Christ, and thinking minds are aware that it is true to this day. There is no reason for the ruling class not to operate out of self-interest unless they have surrendered to a larger Self. It is to the credit of recent democracies that they have been able to convince their people that this is no longer true. It is to the shame of Reagan's America that we no longer even care that we had a president who openly loathed the poor and clothed the rich.

Epitomizing Peck's *People of the Lie,* the Reagans were able to appear God-fearing while never going to church, stand for family values while caring almost nothing about their own, say they were against abortion while risking nothing for its reversal, go on record as being against taxes while in fact increasing hidden taxes thirteen times, get elected on a platform against big government while increasing the deficit more than all presidents put together, and the American people were largely willing to perceive Ronald Reagan as a man of integrity and statesmanship.

That is not so much a judgment on the morality of Ronald Reagan as a judgment on the quality and depth of American religion and American prayer. Religion has been coopted to legitimize and bless the selfish interests of the ruling class, while still daring to pray to the poor man Jesus and still daring to read his sermons in our churches. We can no longer presume that because people go to church they also know how to pray. In fact, one wonders if institutional religion does not more often create its own ruling class—where truth-seeking prayer is almost impossible to happen. When there is too much private soul to protect, the Great Soul cannot be sought.

If religion and religious people are to have any moral credibility in the face of the massive death-dealing and death denial of this century, we need to move with great haste toward lives of *political holiness.*

Christians kneel and raise hands, Buddhists sit in surrender, Muslims bow their heads to the earth many times a day, Natives whirl and dance before the Power, and Hindus burn incense and offer sacrifices. We are all fairly consistent with our rituals. We defend them and too often identify with them. But now we must go beyond the defended ritual to the Reality for which it stands. This is my theology and my politics:

It appears that God loves life: The creating never stops.
We will love and create and maintain life.
It appears that God is love—an enduring, patient kind.
We will seek and trust love in all its humanizing (and therefore divinizing) forms.
It appears that God loves variety, feature, many faces and forms.
We will not be afraid of the other, the not-me, the stranger at the gate.
It appears that God loves—*is*—beauty: Look at this world!
Those who pray already know this. Their passion will be for beauty.
They don't need religion or this article. The fire and the flesh are already One.

Part III

TO WALK HUMBLY WITH YOUR GOD

Mending The Breach: 1993 Theme

RICHARD ROHR, OFM

The ancient ruins will be rebuilt,
You will build on age-old foundations.
You will be called "Breach-Menders,"
And "Restorer of ruined houses."

Isa. 58:12

I am wondering if I have ever understood faith—or if I want it now that I am getting the point. The price of faith is much higher than I imagined it to be in my youthful readings about martyrdoms and lives of heroic sacrifice.

Now I know that faith is *not* believing-certain-ideas-all-evidence-to-the-contrary. It is not dogged loyalty to childhood conditioning or pledges of allegiance to sacred formulas and official explanations. It is surely not the addictive repetition of rituals or practices that keep God under control. These approaches give the ego comfort, but they give little comfort to truth and even less to the scary and wonderful coming of the Reign of God.

I can only describe faith in its effects: People of real faith seem able to hold increasing amounts of chaos in one tranquil and ordered life. Faith seems to make people spacious, noncontrolling, and waiting in awareness. The faith that Jesus praises as salvation and sufficient in lepers, Samaritans, and those outside the temple system is something very different from religion as such. It is a capacity within people to contain and receive all things, to hold onto nothing, with almost no need to fear or judge rashly. Faith people find it unnecessary to secure themselves because they are secure at a deeper level. There is room for another in that spacious place.

If Someone is not holding together the Big World, then I had best concentrate on making sense out of my own little corner. If No One else is finally in charge, I had best take charge. If No One else is caring for me, I had better be preoccupied with security and insurance. If No One else is naming me, I will be very invested in my own image. If the only joy is self-acquired, then any mood-altering substance will do. All the burden, anxiety, and options are back on me, and I *must* take myself too seriously. It is the glory and the price of secular men and women. When Prometheus can no longer enjoy sitting at the fireplace of the gods, he must steal his own fire, but he pays the price forever. Such seems our contemporary exile. The human mind is enamored and burdened with itself, trying desperately to hold itself together. Trapped in our fractured worlds, we are unable to reconnect with one another.

Because people of faith are comfortable with the totality, they are the only ones who can hold the disparate parts together, make the peace, or, as we are saying this year, "mend the breach." More than ever, we think that is our task here at CAC. The recurring temptation is to separate, analyze, and judge the parts, which gives us a sense of control and "understanding." But Steve Levine speaks universal wisdom when he declares that "understanding is the ultimate seduction of the mind. Go to the truth beyond the mind. Love is the bridge." Faith, driven by love, gives up its need to understand, lets go, and allows Someone else to hold us together. It is not giving up as much as opening up—and refusing to close back down for the sake of self-sufficiency and mastery. If this is indeed the character of faith for postmodern people, or any people, then I finally know why faith is so rare and why Jesus himself wondered if he would find very much on this earth (Luke 18:8).

Today there seems to be a breach in almost every wall. Some have said, the "cosmic egg" that seemed to hold us together for a long time is now broken: "All the king's horses and all the king's men" find themselves unable to put it back together again. It feels as if the earth moved beneath us somewhere in the mid or late sixties: the old certitudes, the agreed-upon assumptions, the core values of Western civilization came up for major questioning. Our presuppositions dissolved, and the questioning has not stopped for twenty-five years. We now find ourselves engaged in major and sometimes minor culture wars on almost every personal and social issue. Mario Cuomo and Patrick Buchanan represent not just different political parties. They are coming from utterly different symbolic universes—yet they both were raised Catholic and American! It is all thinkable now, and most of us are beyond being shocked by anything. We are often sad, discouraged, and even alienated from the only world we have. It was so much easier to live inside the cosmic egg! It feels like exile from home and it manifests in rampant abuse, violence, victim behavior, denial, social hysteria, or lifeboat ethics. Each enclave of security seems to be clutching at its small certitudes: defiant, assertive, and substituting opinions for deeper identity.

We yearn for breach-menders who can restore our ruined houses, as Isaiah says. We long for great-souled people who can hold the chaos together within themselves—and give us the courage to do the same. In mythology this is the gift of the queen or the king. In religion it is symbolized by the temple in Jerusalem or the cathedral at the center of the city. In the psychological world, we speak simply of mental and emotional health. In spirituality, we dare to long for God. But our condition instead is always one of exile. We are "pilgrims and strangers on this earth" (Heb. 11:13). It was in exile that Jewish religion attained its most mature state. Out of exile, Second Isaiah took religious poetry and prophecy to its height. The collectivist ethics of Israel were refined and personalized by Jeremiah and Ezekiel, and the story of Job emerged to push the meaning of faith beyond conventional wisdom. Maybe it is the necessary pattern. Eliphaz, Bildad, and Zophar were good religious men, giving Job the traditional religious advice, but it was still insufficient. Exile led Israel to the edges of what it had already experienced and battered open the door to the new realm of faith, which is always more than conventional wisdom. We are in cultural and spiritual exile in America now, and we long to return to Jerusalem (or even Kansas!). Maybe a new door needs to be opened.

I doubt whether a single cultural myth or national story is now possible. That is frightening as we experience the fractured results while groups divide, encircle, and defend: male versus female, rich versus poor, liberal versus conservative, Christian versus non-Christian, pro-life versus pro-choice, renew from within versus change from without, overdeveloped world versus underdeveloped world, straights versus gays, environmentalists versus developers, hierarchies versus memberships, whites versus people of color . . . The rifts and chasms are irreparable. Many are unable to offer one another basic respect, engage in civic dialogue, or honor what God is apparently patient with: the human struggle. The Catholic Church is in disbelief and panic at its inability to be a truly universal communion. But I am still advised by Thomas Aquinas, who said, "We must love them both: those whose opinions we share and those whose opinions we reject. For both have labored in search for their truth and both have helped us in the finding of our own."

For the middle part of this century the goal seemed to be integration, homogenization, centralization, uniformity for the sake of unity, upward mobility, and acceptance. Suddenly the pattern is reversing worldwide. Is it the impossibility of the task? The failures along the way? The phenomena of Russia, the Baltics, the Berlin Wall? Now the words are "multiculturalism," diversity, smaller units, ethnic identity, decentralization, states' rights, and my rights. For such a paradigm shift we need a new ethic and vision for ourselves. If it was *e pluribus unum* ("out of the many, one") for the past two hundred years in the U.S., it now feels like *ex uno multos* ("out of the one, *many*"). How do you create a new cultural myth when you are now many cultures and also shifting into a seemingly reverse speed? Such is our problem.

The overriding temptation of both churches and nations today is to circle their wagons and worship their own Promethean fire. But the ancient ruins must be built on age-old foundations: We need to assert both exclusivity and inclusivity, both priesthood and prophecy, both identity and universal table fellowship, both holding on and letting go, both the nuclear family and global consciousness. The conservative temptation is to put all the energy into the first: Batten down the hatches! The liberal temptation usually succumbs to the second: No boundaries are worth defending except the right to choose itself.

We both need to recognize our underlying cultural assumptions, the "myths" out of which we all operate. Until we can admit that largely nonrational myths guide and determine our so-called rational choices, there is little chance that we will "restore the ruined houses" of our civilization. Until we each own our biases, love and human community will be for the inner circle only. Such love is pretty feeble, if it is love at all. Skinhead loyalties and mafioso charity do not make the world go 'round. Charity begins at home, but it does not end there.

Come join us during any or all of our "Mending the Breach"

programs in 1993. We hope to do what we can to demilitarize the culture wars by facilitating a year of dialogue, information, understanding, and healing prayer. Come help us understand one another in a dark time, and push back the constricted edges of our faith.

Becoming an Active Contemplative

CHRISTINA SPAHN

Several years ago, while on retreat, I saw a poster that has remained the most lasting image of that time. The poster featured a massive St. Bernard, head hung forlornly over the wooden gate. Captioning the picture were these words: "I've tried so hard to be what others said I should be, I've forgotten who I really am."

There are a few of us who, at least in times of graced vulnerability, cannot identify with the confusion, self-alienation, and disillusionment of those words. From infancy on, we have been conditioned to think of ourselves in terms of the roles appropriate to us, to compare ourselves with others, to judge our worth by what we do, what we have, what we accomplish, and the affirmation we received. Identifying so completely with roles, expectations, affirmed qualities, and those "negative" characteristics we allow into consciousness, it's not surprising that we think their sum total is who we truly are.

This became painfully clear to me personally in the process of leaving a religious community of which I'd been a member for twenty-one years. Giving up the title *Sister* was extremely difficult—not because I used it often but because it had become a self-identification for who I thought I was and how I wished to be seen by others. Yet, it was only in surrendering this image that I've learned other things about myself, things to which I hopefully cling a little less tenaciously because in time they too will need to be surrendered.

In speaking to Cistercian novices, Thomas Merton once said,

"The fundamental truth you have to face is your own falsity. We have to begin by accepting the truth of our falsity. As soon as I grasp this, I'm on the right way." It's important to note that Merton says nothing about fixing, changing, or bemoaning this falsity. He simply counsels its recognition and acceptance.

Recognizing, accepting, and being with our falsity and, paradoxically, with our truth is a primary aspect of contemplative prayer. Because this form of prayer is without words, images, thoughts, or feelings, it's not easily hooked by an ego constantly on the look for further aggrandizement. Minus the masks, roles, and illusions that protect us from ourselves and each other, the contemplative simply *is,* and in that very is-ness recognizes emptiness and Fullness, poverty and Bounty, self and God, knowing these not as distinct but as one: truth in Truth, light in Light.

As contemplative prayer leads to union with God, it intrinsically and invariably leads to union with all people and all creation. That is why the work of prayer and the work of justice are so essentially related. One cannot truly know God and self in the silence of personal prayer without also knowing God and self in the suffering, anguish and despair of humanity and our violated earth. The only appropriate response to such knowing is involvement.

The Center has affirmed the integration of action and contemplation. In a dualistic world, where things are too often seen as either/or, we need to avoid looking at these as separate polarized realities. To be active *and* contemplative is very different from being active contemplatives. While the first involves a frequently uneasy truce between what might superficially appear irreconcilable opposites, the second involves integration of both in such a way that the meaning of each is immeasurably enhanced. Integrating action and contemplation is much more than simply giving due time to each—although that time is essential. Rather, integration demands engagement open to the conversion possibilities of both so that, as personally enfleshed, action and contemplation become indistinguishable.

The process of becoming an active contemplative, what Jesus was and what each of us is called to be, is the work of a lifetime—a work that is not the individual's but God's. The only thing we can do, and that too is graced, is simply give ourselves to the process. Reading, workshops, and so on, are helpful, but more important than anything we know and understand is commitment to daily practice—in silence, in awareness, and in response to the here and now situation. This requires neither monastic schedules nor academic degrees. Instead, it demands the humility to live reflectively but not take ourselves too seriously, the discipline of daily contemplative prayer (even when it's "boring"—and it sometimes is!), a wholehearted and enthusiastic participation in all we do, and the courage to witness countercultural values since we will be increasingly unwilling to play the games through which the American illusion survives. One becomes an active contemplative by being one. There is no other way.

Reconstruction

RICHARD ROHR, OFM

Many conversations and meetings of the last year have led me to some clarifying but also disturbing conclusions. In very brief form, I would like to share these with you. They might be helpful in responding to our "Mending the Breach" question. I know they are providing me with some long-sought direction, and I hope they can do the same for the readers of *Radical Grace*.

It has become evident to many of us that Western civilization is in the midst of a major "crisis of meaning." All of our institutions are suffering. For the past few years I have been quoting Joseph Chilton Pearce, who speaks of the "cracking of the cosmic egg." Now I am beginning to see how truly devastating that crack is. The symbolic universes inside of which we lived safely have largely fallen apart, leaving only the private psyche on its lonely journey toward meaning. Mary Jo Leddy, who taught brilliantly at our summer peace and justice conference, said that all we have left is mere "episodic meaning." There is no larger mythic story that explains our lives, and each day we must create some personal moment to make ourselves feel significant or even alive. Often this is merely therapy or victimhood. Without sacred mythology, all we have left is private pathology: my little story disconnected from any group story and surely disconnected from any Great Story. That is a lonely and tragic way to live. It is therefore not surprising that we have so many angry and cynical people in the West today, often looking for someone to blame for their unhappiness. Usually the blame goes to those who supposedly have the power, which locks us into the role of the powerless.

Apparently we are at the long end of what philosophers call "deconstructionism." It began with the Enlightenment, the critical rationalism of the eighteenth century, and has continued in various forms of skepticism and sophistry leading to the wholesale "politics of suspicion" that we live today. We are all affected by it to some degree, and it has surely aided us in being more self-critical and rightly critical of ailing beliefs and institutions. The trouble is that you cannot live on criticism; you surely cannot build anything communal when you start with negation, and finally criticism gives no joy to the present and no hope to the next generation. Behaviorally, it is the opposite of faith and often creates in its participants a sort of antifaith—toward everything. Now I can see why we proclaim the Creed at the middle of the Christian liturgy (what we *do* believe), as opposed to the whining and complaining that characterizes so many gatherings today (what we are against, what has hurt us, who is wrong, and why we should sue!). Something tells me that this is a culture in serious decline and a people who have nothing to believe in. "Without vision, the people will surely perish" (Prov. 29:18).

Even the much appreciated "Recovery Movement" seems to assume that there is a previous wholeness to recover to! Ideological feminism has often deconstructed the last four thousand years of civilization with a kind of reverse messianism that presumes all was well and good when women ran the world. Unfortunately there is no one around to prove it. New Agers and advocates of Native spiritualities are "committed" to religions for which there is no accountability but only dreamy private revelations to be used at will. All of which drives the old holders of the Western myth (Judeo-Christianity) into reactionary fundamentalism and rigid orthodoxy. All of us, with no "One God before us," no agreed-upon accountable values, now righteously hold one another accountable in ways that would make the old patriarchs wince! Just witness the absolutism and final judgments in present-day political correctness. There is no longer any "mortal sin" in a deconstructed society, but suddenly words like "appalled," "outraged," "violated," and "raped" are common parlance. "Insensitivity" is the cover-all sin by which the new liberal can control and convict you better than any bully pulpit ever did. All in the name of peace and justice, of course. I suspect that the next generation will not hate the clergy and the establishment so much; they will just hate one another—for all the betrayals, accusations, gossip, arraignments, and unforgiveness. Maybe what law and pyramid did was protect us from the invisible poison of unaccountable persons and circles.

As a worldview, deconstructionism refuses any accountability to any outer criteria. There is only the private psyche and its personal experience, its rights, and its feelings. There is little ability to appeal to what Vaclav Havel, the poet-president of the Czech Republic, calls "a politics of meaning ... not the art of the useful, but politics as practical morality, in service to the truth." There is no objective meaning out there for the true deconstructionist. There is no scale by which cultures, ideas, persons, and moralities can be measured. It's finally a jungle of competing rights, and the recent fad or the most powerful/articulate group wins. There is little that is "civil" about it, and one wonders how we will create a great civilization. Everything is "merely," "only," "culturally or gender biased," "relative," or "that's what you are free to think." The very use of the word "truth" is a bit of an embarrassment to a liberal, presuming that the word could only come from a right-wing idiot. The result is the dismissal of most great ideas, centuries of Western philosophy, lifetimes of sanctity, sincere folks who have taken the time to do their intellectual and spiritual homework—all in favor of recent American dissatisfaction with the universe. They forget that even the appeal to a "sin" like insensitivity has no validity unless one accepts the Judaeo-Christian ethic (or some ethic) in the first place. If the deconstructionist is consistent, he or she moves toward the nihilism that we are roundly experiencing in relationships, morality, art, and government today.

One wonders if America has basically become ungovernable. If the only appeal is to private rights and privilege, I predict that we will elect a new party and president every four years. Most forget that Aristotle said democracy would only work in a culture already committed to virtue. There is no communal myth left that teaches us the essentially tragic nature of human life; there is no vision that proclaims the primacy of the common good; there is no transcendent image that makes human virtue a divine reflection. There is No One to reflect and No One to love and serve. I do not want to belong to a religion that cannot kneel. I do not want to live in a world where there is No One to adore. It is a lonely and labored world if I am its only center. My life is too short to discover wisdom on my own, to identify and properly name my own self-importance, to learn how to love if I have to start at zero.

I am especially impassioned about the next generation. They seem to have nothing. We have given them less than crumbs, only our own criticism and cynicism about things. As much as I have given my own priesthood to work for reform and change, I must admit that this does little of itself to inspire, transform or unite. It does not of itself point toward Someone to adore, something worth living for, and some things worth dying for. As Vaclav Havel also says, all we have left in the West are "things worth buying." More liberal reforms, all the married and women priests in the world, will not fill the enormous spiritual vacuum of the young—or the old, for that matter. Our people are dying for lack of vision, for lack of transcendent meaning to name their soul and their struggles. What good is inclusive language if no one is even listening to our message? Why would a young person join a group of fifty-year-old complainers who are unwilling to speak of God and joy and peace beyond comprehension? These are the obsessive preoccupations of my generation who have had more freedom, change, our-way-of-arranging-the-world, than any generation in human history. Why are we unwilling to join in the cosmic dance that invites and thrills the would-be searchers? Why are so many of us, deconstructed more than we are aware, afraid to kneel and adore what is—in the only lifetime we will ever have? Don't we know, in the words of Anne Lamott, that a hundred years from now it will be "all new people"? We must give them something good to build on.

I think it is time for reconstruction. We need to know what we *do* believe, why we are proud of our-only-past, what is good about even the broken things (life, church, state), and how we can begin a new language of responsibility. At this point, I think anything else is a waste of time and refusal of grace. Human life is too short to waste it on the negative. It is too easy to be cynical.

I commit whatever years I have left to *reconstruction* (Not regression or rigidity!) of a church and culture of meaning. Otherwise we will have no positive alternative ready when the deconstructed system falls apart. I have no doubt that it will, because love is always stronger than death.

True Traditionalism: Who Will Be Foolish Enough?

RICHARD ROHR, OFM

*M*y fear and dread is that this generation might have to pass from leadership before we can reconstruct. Yet I know that the reconstructionists are already being formed and are surely already among us. Those who will lead into the future will have some hard-won virtues that I will try to describe here. But there is one character type that we cannot do without. Those who name and exemplify what God is doing will be "holy fools."

By the holy fool I mean what Bible and mythic literature have always presented as the "savior." They are persons who are *happily, but not naively, innocent of everything that the rest of us take for granted.* They alone can trust and live the new work of God because they are not protecting the past by control (conservatives) or reacting against the past by fixing (liberals). Both of these are too invested in their own understanding to let go and let God do something new on earth:

> Bring forward the people that is blind, yet has eyes,
> that is deaf and yet has ears . . .
> No need to recall the past,
> No need to think about what was done before.
> See, I am doing something new!
> Even now before it comes to light, can you not see it?
>   Isaiah 43:8, 18–19, written in exile

According to pattern, the wise fools are always formed in the testing ground of exile when the customary and familiar are taken away and they must go much deeper and much higher for wisdom. As a result, they no longer fit or belong among their own. Yet they alone can point the way to the ever new Jerusalem. Conventional wisdom is inadequate, even if widely held by good people. Thus it is only Parsifal, the "perfect fool," who can find the path to the Holy Grail. It is Paul, isolated but enthralled by a vision of universal Gospel, who can say:

> Make no mistake about it: if you think you are wise, in the ordinary sense of the word, then *you must learn to be a fool* before you can really be wise. (1 Cor. 3:18)

It is Jeremiah the prophet who can see his undershorts as an image of the bonding and bridge to God (Jer. 13:1–11). It is Ezekiel who can play children's games and mimes in the streets (Ezekiel 4:1–5:4), even though he is a priest of the Temple. It is Trudy, the bag lady in Lily Tomlin's *The Search for Signs of Intelligent Life in the Universe*, who experiences Plato's holy madness, "a divine release of the soul from the yoke of custom and convention." Trudy says that what we call reality is "the leading cause of stress among those in touch with it."

The holy fool today is the full feminist who can tell her sisters that they have bypassed the great compassion for the sake of mere ideology. The holy fool today is Cornel West, the Black intellectual, who can tell his own people that they are "preoccupied with 'getting over'—with acquiring pleasure, property and power by any means necessary." The holy fool today is Rosemary Haughton, who can write an entire book on the magnificence of *The Catholic Thing* while the rest of us clutch to our private hurts like sulking teenagers. The holy fool today is Daniel Nichols, the conservative Catholic, who can tell his fellow papists that 'individual responsibility cannot be dismissed by some exaggerated notion of authority." The holy and wise fool today is anyone who can open up new, uncharted and sure-to-be criticized territory—beyond "the narrow framework of the dominant liberal and conservative views, which with its worn-out vocabulary leaves us intellectually debilitated, morally disempowered, and personally depressed" (Cornel West). The holy and wise fool today is Beatrice Bruteau, the Christian philosopher and contemplative in North Carolina. She knows all the garbage, scandals, and hypocrisy of the day and still proclaims "Radical Optimism."

The holy fool is the last stage of the wisdom journey. It is the man or woman who knows his or her dignity and therefore does not have to polish or protect it. It is the man or woman who has true authority and does not have to defend it or anyone else's authority. It is the child of God who has met the One who "hurls galaxies and watches over sparrows" (Greg Flannery) and therefore can comfortably be a *child* of God. These, and these alone, can be trusted to proclaim the Reign of God. The rest of us will merely deconstruct, trapped in our own self-serving pain. Most will just try to get through another day.

It has taken most of my life to see that faith is finally the freedom to smile, relax, and see that it is *ok* anyway; to stop controlling, fixing, explaining, needing, changing—while still doing what I can for justice and peace. I have had enough of morbid activists, politically correct Vatican II liberals, and enlightened minds who have lost their souls. It took me a long time to see the difference between love and mere power. I do not want a pope who can't smile. Nor do I trust others who can't smile. The fragile language of "Be good to yourself," "I deserve this," "I am offended by," and "I have a right to" is too easy, petty, and untested by time. It is hard to believe that such small and cautious voices will ever be holy fools who can reconstruct anything.

Many of my friends and readers have been surprised how critical I have been of the current, psychologically correct style. They wonder why I am so pessimistic about liberals when they always thought that I was one. Let me try to define and clarify what I mean by recent American liberalism. Maybe that will help explain my stand.

By liberalism I mean a contemporary mindset that has been formed by lots of freedom, lots of education, and lots of seeming progress. It puts all its hope and trust in these things. The uncritical starting point is the individual and his or her "truth" and development. There is usually a visionary or romantic notion of the common good, but little actual willingness to surrender personal freedoms for the sake of a public morality, a public church, or a public anything. Here the conservatives are clearly more defensible in theory even though their jargon does not always translate into critical public policy. And many contemporary conservatives are, in fact, liberals because they usually sell out to the private self when their own privileges are called into question. True traditionalists, philosophically grounded and consistent, are actually rather unusual today. Our education system is not rigorous enough to produce them. Mario Cuomo, Mary Jo Leddy, and Vaclav Havel would perhaps be examples.

Media-formed liberals are dedicated to ending our captivity to fate, custom, and coercion—and calling that freedom. They seek the ideal person, cause, or idea (usually a personal feeling) to believe in. They work tirelessly for change and growth of persons, causes, and ideas—so that they *can* believe in them. Predictably, the disillusionment and burnout rate is very high. They are in love with being in love. They are in love with the rightness, the smoothness, the order, the clarity, the workability of things—and not really things as they are: unfixed, broken, poor, and partly right. Normally liberals do not have the humility or the patience to be a part of that which they consider beneath them: institutions, church, history, and especially conservatives. The way through, I think, is for both to trust *true traditionalism,* while interpreting tradition in alive and creative ways.

It has become unrealistic to expect solutions from the gradual evolution of liberal values and institutions. They are too tied to individual rights, market values, media-formed "feelings," and mere utilitarian goals. Most are "reeds shaking in the wind," but with just enough educated language to appear planted and committed. My experience is that such liberals never stay in for the long haul or build things that last.

The best that such people will create are well-oiled and up-to-date bureaucracies, "which are never uninvented once they are adopted." The emphasis is upon division of labor, hierarchy of accountability, written procedures, job descriptions, consistency, precedent setting, fairness, separation of office from personality, universality of treatment, justification of policy, and the inviolability of agreed-upon process. Without such things, we remain small, contentious, and ineffective today. These things protect us from one another and from the institution itself. But it is the difference between the sweep and grandeur of the Acts of the Apostles and the plodding concerns of the pastoral letters to Timothy and Titus. The first is open missionary theology and evangelization; the second is "residential theology," the necessary follow-up. The first is

Exodus, the second is Leviticus and Numbers. The trouble is that both are in the Bible. Holy fools must serve and respect the royal court; the kings and queens must protect and allow the fool to be heard.

Spiritual goals and values, charisma and holy foolishness tend to lose out in the bureaucratic model, even though it also provides a way to test and refine the prophetic word. Normally it takes great humility, persistent advocacy, and the surrender of turf to admit disruptive truth from outside the agreed-upon loop and the salaried professionals. Institutions are always both resource and problem. The holy fool must always be allowed to reveal and topple the idolatry of system. Thus St. Paul, the archetypal outsider, must be raised up by God to broaden the perspective of the twelve apostles themselves. But before he raises him up, God throws him down on the Damascus road. The holy fool must not *need* to be the holy fool too much. He must be purified, humbled, freed from small mind and stingy heart. He has to be a team player, patient with incarnation and human structure. He has to be willing to work with the pedestrian concerns of Timothy and Titus. Maybe that is what finally refines and teaches compassion to the holy fool. The wise and holy fool will always be a fire-tested alloy of spirit, soul, and embodiment: trapped in none of them, awake to all three.

Let's try briefly to list the essential characteristics of reconstructionists:

1) A preparedness to be positive/A deep Yes to what is.
2) A vision of the Whole/Communitarian values (which include the weakest)
3) A passion for the next generation
4) A sense of limits/humility/self-control
5) A willingness to carry the dark side of self, others, and history
6) A reverence for the past; for tradition; for ancestors
7) A capacity to be critical/Resistance to idolatries and patriotisms
8) A soulful and embodied approach to religion/Going beyond mere mind and spirit
9) A sufficient freedom from private ego and personal agenda
10) A growing trust in God as security, grace, and mercy.

I am quite content with these weaknesses ... for it is when I am weak that I am strong. Now I have been talking like a fool, but you forced me to do it.

Paul to his reconstructionists
in Corinth (2 Cor. 12:10–11

Making Space For Blue

AVIS CROWE

*T*he eye of a hurricane is that peculiar phenomenon of stillness at the center of the storm's destructive turbulence. I have used this as a metaphor: When the whole world seems to be running amok, it helps to think that I might stand in the middle of it and not be destroyed or, more likely, tempted into despair. But beyond that I never really thought about it—until writer Phillip Hallie helped me to move more deeply into the metaphor by providing me with an image that I carry in my heart and can draw on when the world is too much with me.

Hallie is the author of *Lest Innocent Blood Be Shed,* the book that documents the remarkable story of a tiny village in France that provided safe haven for Jews during the Nazi occupation. I saw him interviewed on public television. I've long since forgotten the larger context of the program, but the writer made one brief observation that immediately captured my attention. He said, "There is a space in the middle of a hurricane where the sky is blue and birds sing." What a powerful image that is for me! It isn't just that it is calm, which could as well be a dead calm, simply a lack of turbulence; but Hallie painted that space with broader strokes, creating a picture of beauty, of color and sound, of life.

One can easily hang out a laundry list of societal ills, issues that cry out for solution yet only seem to worsen with time. I recently had a conversation with a man who can find nothing to affirm in our culture. A veteran of years of political organizing, peace activism, and prophetic witness, he is tired of whistling in the wind when no one is willing to listen, and all he can see is our relentless drive toward more and more and more until we drive ourselves out of existence. As he spoke, I found myself taking on the weight of his distress, the color of his despair. Yet I resist acknowledging the reality of much of what he says. It's true that at almost every turn there are reasons to throw in the towel. The ranks of the homeless swell daily. An acquaintance spoke of an altercation with her daughter's wedding caterer and the likelihood of having to have legal assistance to recoup the $2,600 deposit they had put down . . . this when thousands of our neighbors haven't enough food to put on the table. Our insistence on living "the good life" defined by VCRs, microwaves, CD players, and houses with enough room to shelter several families brings with it awesome consequences. How is it possible to see beauty, to laugh, to remain centered in the midst of life's turbulence? Yet as someone called to a faith-filled, contemplative approach to life, that is precisely what I am invited to do.

The most storm-tossed may be closest to that patch of blue Hallie described and can help us see it, to trust that it is there, to keep our eye and heart on the sky and the birdsong, even when we are surrounded by the storm. An important companion on my own journey is Etty Hillesum, the young woman whose journals, *An Interrupted Life,* document a growing faith in God even as she moved closer to her own death in Auschwitz. Though a member of a privileged family who could have escaped internment, Etty chose not to avoid the fate of so many. She volunteered to go to one of the camps to help her people. There she worked in the hospital, became message-bearer for many, and wrote about the life she and others experienced. She understood well what was happening as she watched family and friends transported to Auschwitz and certain death. Etty accepted the likelihood of her own fate. Through all of this her faith deepened.

As I read Etty's words I can almost see her peeling away the layers, coming to a clarity of thought, vision, and hope that is as awesome as it is difficult to comprehend. Close to the end of her life, she could still write, "There will always be a small patch of sky above, and there will always be enough space to fold two hands in prayer." Etty Hillesum was a woman who made space for blue, and who shows me that it is possible, even essential, if I am to live the kind of full, meaningful, and generous life I aspire to.

I've not been tested in the same dramatic way as Etty and so many others I've had the privilege of knowing in difficult places like rural Georgia and South Africa. Yet I do know, like most people, the truth of a phrase an aunt of mine used to use: "Life is so daily!" I fall prey to periodic bouts of sadness, melancholy, and anger over storms of my own making or the more violent storm of suffering, indifference, and greed swirling all around me. Now and then a headline or a story on the news or a painful, unhealed recollection from the past will wash over me in waves of gray or even black. But I know I have a choice. I do not have to give in to despair. I can know that truth of what is all around me and still choose to celebrate life and all its possibility. I am grateful to Phillip Hallie and Etty Hillesum for giving me an image that I can call upon to bring me back to blue.

Professionalism and Violence

MIKE ROCHE

*F*or three weeks last summer my fourteen-year-old son and I worked with a group of Global Volunteers teaching English to adolescents in rural Poland. Each volunteer was assigned a group of four to seven youths to meet with daily for three hours of formal instruction. Informal activities were scheduled throughout the remainder of the days and evenings. Since no one in our corps of volunteers possessed significant experience in teaching English as a second language, we each approached our responsibilities with considerable anxiety, few expectations, very little in terms of professional models or jargon, but also with infectious enthusiasm and great commitment. I'm still trying to figure out how we were able to learn so much from each other, have so much fun, and feel so much love. I hope some of my reflections during our three weeks and following our visit to a radically different kind of camp—

Auschwitz—have relevance to our understanding of professionalism and violence.

My group of students consisted of four boys, ages seven, ten, twelve and fourteen. After the first forty-five minute introductory session with Stashek, Piotrek, Marchen, and Marek, I wrote in my journal: "It was a test getting through our time today and it was only forty-five minutes! I'm going to have to be very resourceful to fill our time together. 'Professor' crutches won't hold me up here." In fact, I didn't "fill" our time together, even though it would have been a very professional thing to try to do. It wasn't that I didn't want to control and fill our time; I just didn't have the skills or techniques necessary to pull it off. Since I was incapable of "seizing" each day. I had little choice but to open myself to receive the mysteries each one had to offer. We used poems and prayers, songs and dances, and our laughter and our tears at the end of the camp to "talk" with one another. The conversation was deep. It allowed us to get underneath surface differences of nationality, age, religion, and the like to a place where we were together in a way that was hardly at all apart.

As my affection for my students grew with each day, I was reminded of the stories my wife shares with me of her years as a grade school teacher. I often marvel at the intensity of her feelings and the clarity of recollection she has for events that involved students she instructed over twenty years ago. Compared to this grade school teacher, I wondered why so few of the professors I know have so few cherished recollections of time spent with their students. After my Polish experience, I am convinced that part of the explanation lies in the fact that my wife's role as a grade school teacher was not nearly as confining as that of the typical professor. Living together in the classroom and the bathroom, at breakfast and lunch, through recess and school programs, and while on the bus and at the zoo creates infinite opportunities for individual stories to weave together to produce rich fabrics of purpose, hope, and community. In our small group of four Polish boys and one American man, I know that as we were stumbling through "Six Little Ducks That I Once Knew" in preparation for the camp variety show, we were also stumbling toward one another and exploding the standard roles and patterns of small self that kept us apart. I started scribbling in my journal about how tiny little definitions of professional "self" can distance us from one another, reduce our effectiveness, and, perhaps in some sense, even result in the perpetration of violence.

And then we went to Auschwitz. The teachers went without the students on a weekend toward the end of the camp. I thought I was prepared for horrible, but how could I have been ready for a room full of beautiful hair shorn from women on their way to the gas chambers? How could I have been ready for a room filled with bent and broken spectacles that allowed terrified eyes to view what most of the world refused to see? How could I have been ready for a room filled with thousands of shoes or the displays of infant clothing? How could I have been ready to stand next to the ovens used to incinerate the holy bodies of some 1.5 million victims? How could I have been ready to observe photographs such as the one of a young German officer crouched in preparation to shoot a fleeing mother desperately clutching her infant child? I was not ready; I never want to be ready. I never want to be able to understand fully what Heinrich Himmler meant when, in speaking to his concentration camp subordinates, he explained that "what makes us great is our ability to do this necessary work and still go home at night and be decent fathers and husbands." Himmler is the one who got me thinking about professionalism again.

I began to see Himmler as presenting a grotesque example of "professional" distance. He defined greatness according to how unaffected and removed he could become from the hair, the glasses, the shoes, the infants' clothing, and the evil odor of extermination. Since his profession was murder, I can understand how distance from his victims could greatly enhance his "productivity." I have a much more difficult time understanding the logic of professional distance as it applies to counselors, clergy, doctors, nurses, lawyers, teachers, police officers, probation officers, and any other profession that brings people into frequent contact with each other. I know that the dominant tradition in the American professions argues that a professional should maintain "detachment" from his or her clients, but my experience tells me that in this context, detachment too often translates into distance and distance produces violence. I speak here not only of violence in its most extreme Himmler form, but of any act that diminishes, victimizes, or objectifies another person. The violent purpose of the death camp is revealed early on in the impersonal numbering of its inmates. But what were doctors-to-be learning when they were told in one recently documented case "You have to learn to treat patients as lab animals"? What did the police who brutalized Rodney King in Los Angeles expose when they referred to him as a "lizard"? And what do professors I have overheard disclose about their mission when they refer to students as "the little shits"? You may say such cases cannot be compared because the purposes of the professions are so dramatically opposed. I believe that although the degree of violence produced may vary, whenever there is distance and objectification, whether the espoused intention is to kill, cure, control, or educate—victimization will be the result. Victimization is the essence of violence. Separation and distance are the essence of evil.

When I picture the detached mechanic who inhabits the role of professional in so many fields, I see a victimizer. When I picture my wife with her grade school students, I see a friend. Thomas Shaffer of Notre Dame has been lobbying for a friendship model of professionals for years. "Friendship is respect for dignity, for personhood, as many modern writers put it—for, as Buber said, the trivial and irreplaceable individual. Friendship as a method makes a skill of concern, of affection, of love." Anthony Padovanco speaks of the imperative nature of this skill. "Nothing reveals itself truly to us until we learn reverence and respect." Feminist authors such as Carol Gilligan and Nel Noddings have also recommended the method of caring, contending that it is most compatible with a feminine way of knowing. According to Noddings, the masculine way of knowing is a detached perspective that focuses on law and principle, whereas the feminine outlook is rooted in receptivity, relatedness, and responsiveness. In a recent article entitled "Caring vs. Curing," Carol Montgomery contends that in her twenty years of psychiatric nursing experience she noticed that "the only time we really made a difference was when we were willing to get involved." Even though our culture's hero stories, celebrate curing rather than caring, Montgomery uses her own and others' research to explore the purpose and effectiveness of a caring approach. "True caring means being willing to step into the background, empowering the patient to heal himself or herself. . . . In a caring encounter, the participants experience union at a level beyond the ego, at the level of the spirit." Montgomery suggests that when our agenda is to fix or cure (and I could add teach, control, punish, and more), the emphasis is on ourselves as ego-heros and the result is likely to be disaster.

More and more I am coming to believe that the cool, detached, professional model too often leads to disaster no matter what the professional relationship is. The problem with those who are firmly attached to the standard image of a professional is that we deeply fear what might be called the loss of illusion of self. We have so much invested in our ego-hero professional roles that it is nearly inconceivable for us to contemplate escape from the confinement of a self-definition that is all we know. From our exiled positions we cannot see the relevance of the African proverb to professional relationships: "A person is a person only through other persons." Parker Palmer's reflections are especially applicable to professionals: "What a curious conception of self we have! We have forgotten that self is a moving intersection of many other selves. We are formed by the lives which intersect with our own." Professionals in every field must make room for these intersections if we wish to be more than mechanics. Professionals in every field must make room for these intersections if we wish to witness growth and healing in ourselves and others. None of us can grow, learn, or heal except in relationships. Professionals must allow for the borders of our "fields" and our "selves" to give way and yield to the truth that "the other person there is thou." As Montgomery puts it: "When we expand our sense of self to include another, we become part of a greater unity, liberating ourselves and our clients from the prison of our isolation."

Above the main gate of the prison that was Auschwitz, through which the inmates passed each day on their way to work, there is a cynical inscription: "Arbeit macht frei." It means "Work will set you free." The inscription told a deadly lie. Love is the only force that has the power to set us free from the prison of our isolation. St. Augustine understood the key to freedom and offered the best motto for professionals that I know: "Love, and do what you like."

For God and Country
and Our Disenchanted Youth

EILEEN BURKE

*T*he church was Gothic but probably neither as large nor cathedral-like as I remember. It could have been any time of the year, but my strongest memories are of fall and winter, kneeling in the dark and chilly building, examining my young soul for occasions of sin.

The values of my childhood encouraged discipline and sacrifice. Examining my behavior during the preceding week, I was much more aware of an obligation not to cause problems for my family than of any concept of parents' unconditional love. The emphasis at church seemed to be on what we owed God rather than what God had given us. Across the street at the public school I attended, the focus was on country rather than God, but the emphasis was the same: what we owed our country as citizens and our obligation to learn. Nobody suggested that school ought to be fun. Most of my classmates were still close enough to an immigrant generation of grandparents to be grateful for a free education and, in those years immediately following World War II, to be confident as we recited "The Pledge of Allegiance" that we were indeed living in a nation "indivisible with liberty and justice for all," a generous country deserving of our love and obedience.

When my own daughters began school, they brought home photocopied worksheets with cute little animals to color. Five frogs plus three frogs equals eight frogs. I cheerfully posted the frogs on the refrigerator. When my younger child complained that there was nothing at church for children, I essentially agreed with her. When either of my children described food I set before them as "Yucky," despite the temptation to echo my mother's words, "Eat it. It's good for your soul," I couldn't. There were too many memories of sitting alone at the table choking down something I disliked.

Now my daughters are approaching graduation from high school. The selfish eighties have become the undefined nineties, and I suspect many parents my age have heard themselves described as a generation of self-indulgent youth who spawned a generation of disenchanted, cynical children.

Both my daughters have told me stories that startle and upset me: teens from well-off families who steal; honor students who cheat to maintain their grade point average so they will be offered scholarships to prestigious universities; a lack of respect for leaders at all levels; a loss of confidence in this country and its political institutions; an atmosphere of rudeness, mean-spirited criticism, and willingness to judge by superficialities.

With all the cynicism that her generation is supposed to possess, my older daughter once declared, "I have hope for the future. Things can't get any worse than they are now."

So now I find myself conducting an adult examination of conscience. To what extent am I personally responsible for the situation? How have I failed this coming generation which, as Richard Rohr has stated, seems to have nothing?

The temptation is to absolve myself of all the blame. After all, I was born during World War II and can still remember those days when the old rules applied. And I would not want to return completely to that time of discipline, unquestioning obedience, and deferred pleasures any more than I would want to replace my daughters' brightly colored frogs with the grim workbooks of my early school years. Although I experienced many doubts along the way, I did all right in finding a balance between discipline and personal freedom, between meeting my needs and respecting those of others.

So where lies the guilt? It lies in my failure and the failure of many adults to fill in the pieces for our children. As we made our way through the second half of this difficult century, religious faith and the accompanying codes of honor and duty no longer were as simple as in our childhood; patriotism was no longer as clear-cut as it was for our parents and grandparents. And so we made concessions.

I still slipped into churches to say prayers during a period when I would no longer attend Mass. I decried involvement in Vietnam but continued to get misty-eyed when I sang "The Star Spangled Banner." I worked diligently for political candidates who stood little chance of winning and always felt awed on election day that after all the speeches had been made, the paid advertisements broadcast and printed, everyone's vote was truly equal. However, I failed to articulate my complex feelings to my children. Perhaps I feared that anything I said would be too confusing and contradictory for them to understand. Perhaps I feared some of my beliefs were old-fashioned and out of touch with political realities. Whatever my reasons, in an era when it was fashionable to point out the hypocrisies of organized religions, the corruptions and inadequacies of all governments, I expressed my share of criticism but, in spite of my mixed feelings, did not offer much hope.

As my daughter described the less than perfect world she is to inherit, she was smiling and seemed to possess a seventeen-year-old's healthy confidence that she can do better. I wonder, to what extent have we projected our middle-aged disillusionment onto our children—looking for evidence of cynicism and defeat and, as usual, blaming the political left for all signs of social disorganization and the political right for standing in the way of our accomplishing the idealistic goals of our youth? To what extent have we failed to encourage our children's enthusiasm for life and their youthful confidence that they can find the solutions that eluded their parents?

At any rate, my daughters and I still talk, sometimes at a deep level. Even when I can justifiably say, "Not now, I'm too busy . . . too tired," I try to explain. In words and concepts that lack precision or certainty, I tell them why I believe in God; what's right about this country; why, in spite of all evidence of human evil, I still have faith.

Spiritual Path to Parenting

MARIA D. HABITO

*T*he other day a friend asked me in conversation, "How do you combine your practice of meditation with full-time parenting?"

My friend's question is an important one and has been a daily challenge for me ever since our little boy, Florian Estanislao, was born a year ago. When I went into labor, the practice that kept me going was not the breathing method that we had been taught in our childbirth classes but the very simple method of focusing on the breath, counting from one to ten. How many Zen retreats had I spent doing nothing but sitting down and counting my breath: one two three . . . ten; one two three . . . for hours and days on end. If I am learning one thing in my life from these retreats, it is this: how to become aware of my breathing in every possible situation.

This sounds all so simple and insignificant. When my five-year-old nephew came to visit from Germany and stayed with us, we had an afternoon when friends came for a meditation session at our house, and he took a curious look at them from outside our window in the yard where he was playing, as they sat inside in silence. "What were all these people doing sitting there and staring at the wall?" he asked me later. "They were learning how to breathe, counting from one to ten," I answered. "What? I don't have to learn that; I know it already!" For a little child, maybe so, but for me, focusing on the breath, not only in formal sitting meditation, but more especially in every kind of activity, is an important point in answering my friend's question.

Long before I even knew that I was going to get married and have children, I happened to come across Tsultrim Allione's book, *Women of Wisdom,* a translation of the biographies of accomplished women teachers in Tibetan Tantric Buddhism. In the introduction the author makes some very insightful observations about motherhood, born out of her own struggle of combining her practice of Tibetan Buddhism with the physical realities of parenting and childcare. Already at that time Allione's ideas on motherhood as a spiritual path made so much sense to me.

One might argue that women should have a spiritual path in which they do not have to remove themselves from their life rhythms in order to practice. I agree with that theoretically, and I would like to see more teachings given that really help in dealing with relationships and childrearing in a positive way. Such things as seeing motherhood as a constant attack on selfishness, an admirable ever-present testing of the Bodhisattva Vow to save all sentient beings before ourselves, provides ground for spiritual development. The path of the mother should be given its deserved value as a sacred and powerful spiritual path. It is infuriating to me when I hear, as I frequently do, a man saying that his wife or mother or someone else "does nothing." When I challenge them on this they say, "Of course I meant nothing in the outside world; they only cook, clean, shop, create atmosphere in the home, provide emotional support, etc." This is obviously a perfect example of a patriarchal value system that would give a secretary credit for doing "something" but not a wife. These values have infiltrated the spiritual path as well, and the tremendous spiritual potential of motherhood as a soteriological path has not been given enough appreciation and support.

After our son Florian was born, I found it impossible to go on with my regular practice of Zen sitting from six to seven in the morning. It was his feeding time, and after he went back to sleep, I would try to use every free moment for the preparation of classes, since I was and still am doing part-time teaching. When he was a few months old, I tried bringing him along to the Meditation Center some evenings, hoping that he would sleep in an adjacent room so I could join the meditation with the others. Not used to the environment, he would remain wide awake, breaking the sacred quietness of the Meditation Hall with his baby sounds, and would finally go to sleep shortly before the meditation period ended. These attempts only resulted in the guilty feeling of having him awakened again as we brought him home by car, and this added to my earlier exasperation at having tried unsuccessfully to get him to sleep earlier. So regular meditation has not really been possible for me, except for ten minutes here and there, every now and then when I have been able to catch the time for it. So the question remains: How then do I pursue motherhood as a spiritual path?

I think that every approach to parenting as a spiritual path has to begin with the realization that the little sentient being entrusted to us is one that calls for spiritual nurturing as well. Common experience tells us that plants wilt if we don't water them enough. In the same way, the invisible spiritual seed dries up if it is not taken care of. It takes more than diapers and milk to nurture this important dimension in an infant's life.

It may sound surprising, but I am convinced that babies already can and do meditate. One of my earliest childhood memories is of sitting in front of a window, waiting for the first snowflakes to cover the dark pines outside, being filled with a sense of longing, mystery, beauty and sacredness. I must have been waiting like that at the beginning of many winters, because the memory and the feelings associated with it are still imprinted on my whole being. I continue to treasure this vivid sense of the mysterious nature that enveloped me in a sacred time and space. At that time nobody interrupted my silent meditation. I didn't have to get up and move, to get ready for day care or preschool. I was simply allowed to be and to be where I longed to be.

I find the same fascination with nature in our little Florian. When he was very small, I used to put his stroller outside in the garden, and he would just say there, watching the trees move and speak to him in the wind. At the age of six months I would ask him: "Florian, where are the trees?" And in response he would look at the trees. Now, a very active crawler, he still likes to sit out there or in front of the window and gaze at the trees. I often join him for a short while, watching the trees together, and I focus on my breathing before turning to the housework.

Housework is where the practice really gets tested, because it is a constant field of action. Here, I draw inspiration not only from Allione's remarks but again from my own practice of sitting meditation that I had more time for before the little one was born.

The retreats I had been used to joining would usually be divided into periods of quiet sitting and periods of "contemplative action" or manual work, such as cleaning the Meditation Hall, corridors, and toilets, or else doing the dishes or working in the garden. The mindfulness and concentration that one develops during the periods of quiet sitting are to be maintained during our daily and very ordinary activities such as doing the dishes and so on.

I remember one incident as I was warming up some milk in the kitchen when the telephone rang in the next room. I rushed to get to the phone, thereby waking up the baby who had been asleep in his cradle and now started screaming. Forgetting about the milk and hoping that Florian would go back to sleep, I tried to listen to what the caller was saying on the phone. But this was also impossible because of my inner restlessness. The smell of the burnt milk finally brought me back to my senses and I excused myself from the caller, rushed back to the kitchen, took the milk from the stove, and rushed to the cradle, rescuing the baby who was just as excited and out of breath as I was. This was certainly not a shining example of the practice of mindfulness.

On one occasion, at the end of a retreat he was directing, Ruben came home and invited me and the baby to go back with him to the meditation center where the participants were waiting for the closing ceremonies. It seems Ruben had told them he would introduce a "new Zen Master" who would join us for these ceremonies. When they saw the three-month-old "Zen Master" in my arms as we entered the Meditation Hall, smiles brightened up their faces.

Ruben was right: Children are our Zen Masters from the first day of their lives. It is almost a mystery to me how much they reflect our own state of mind and emotions. Every mother must have the same experience: If we try to hurry a child because we are in a hurry ourselves, nothing works. The anxiety piles up on both sides, and so it is up to the mother to take a deep breath and not mind missing the beginning of the news or leaving late for an appointment.

The twenty-minute period in the evening when I give Florian his last feeding is also the time for me to sit down and rest, to count from one to ten and relax body and mind. The more focused I am myself, the more easily he goes to sleep. When I find myself thinking about what I have to do after he has gone to sleep, he again grows restless with my own restlessness.

One thing I have learned from Zen retreats is the importance of ritual and rhythm. The fact that every day during a retreat has exactly the same schedule allows the participants to be secure and focused and not to have to worry about what is going to happen next. Trying to give a certain structure or rhythm to every day is just as important in raising a child. In my case, my mother's old-fashioned insistence on having a regular feeding and sleeping schedule for the baby has worked out well. Florian knows his time for meals, play, walk, and sleep and is relaxed as long as not too much is changed. He breathes well and so do I. In a retreat there are good and bad days: days where sitting and breathing are very energizing and days when we think that we are not going to survive one more minute of the same. In "real life" it is similar. But the energies gained in happy and easy days carry us across the more difficult and challenging times of sickness and accidents.

From my experience of many retreats in Germany, Japan, and the United States, I know how people love rituals: the way of bowing when entering the hall, sitting down, and getting up, the way of taking the meals in silence (which is especially ritualized in Japan), the sound of the gong to announce certain hours. Rituals make us more conscious of our own body and mind, of time and space, of our interconnectedness with our fellow beings next to us and out in the world. They instill a sense of harmony, gratitude, and sacredness. Rituals in family life function just the same way.

Recently I met a young mother from my parish who told me in tears that her one-and-a-half-year-old son had just died from falling into a pool. The loss of a child: nothing could be more agonizing, more painful than this. And nothing could be a more challenging spiritual test.

There is a Buddhist story in which the Buddha tells a young woman who has lost her child and is out of her mind with grief to go from house to house and see whether there is a single family who has not yet experienced death. She does so and comes to the realization that death is a reality of existence, just as life is.

For those of us raised in the Catholic tradition, the image of the Pietà, the mother holding her dead child on her lap, speaks to our heart. This is not an image of despair but precisely of hope, right in the midst of our deepest sorrow: that this being we have helped bring forth into the world, nurtured, and gave our own life to is in the hands of God, the source of all life, for all eternity. "It is God who giveth, God who taketh away. Blessed be the name of God." We are invited always to come back to this realization at every moment of our lives: that in everything, in life and death, we are in good hands. Being able to entrust everything upon the Breath, with every moment, gives us this deep assurance.

Finally, I believe that to realize parenthood as a spiritual path doesn't depend on what particular devotion or practice we follow or how much time we are able to devote to these practices. It is the quality of our awareness from day to day that deepens us in this path, helped by our way of entrusting ourselves with each breath in everything we do. And in the end, what counts is how we grow to be more loving and more compassionate in a way that the children given to our care will also become loving and caring human beings.

Not the Center for Activism and Introspection

RICHARD ROHR, OFM

*P*eople have liked and affirmed our long name since the beginning. It was cumbersome but also descriptive and up-front. We hoped it would keep us honest and force us toward balance and ongoing integration. No one could meaningfully disagree with the stated goal. It was classic and rather universal spiritually.

But after four years I have reason to believe that some might agree with the title for the wrong reasons. Activists can see our name as an affirmative of their agenda and introverts can use it to affirm quiet time, not working, and leisure-class navel-gazing. Neither is the delicate balance and art that we are hoping for.

Action as we are using the word does not mean activism, busyness, or do-goodism. Action, however, does mean a decisive commitment toward involvement and engagement in the social order. Issues will not be resolved by mere reflection, discussion, or even prayer. God "works together with" (Rom. 8:28) all those who love. To requote so many saints, "We must work as if it all depends on us and pray as if it all depends on God." That does not imply frenetic programming, but it does say that our work is essential and even cocreative of the new world. Our action is apparently important and dignified in God's eyes. In a real sense we even have a bias toward action (as signified in its placement first in our name), because there is no reason to believe that God gives us anything that we have not said *yes* to by work, decision, and effort.

By activism I mean a preference for one style of social ministry, which usually includes public advocacy, community organization, protests, and perhaps even civil disobedience for the purposes of Gospel and justice. Although we would often support such efforts, we would also encourage that such efforts be planned, prayed over, and discerned in a group. Furthermore, we would be anxious to note that activism as such is not the only or always the best form of social ministry. It must be lived in balance with (1) hands-on immediate service to the needy and (2) efforts to empower, educate, heal, and transform persons. These, together with front line involvement, constitute a full social ministry. Most of us are gifted for one or the other. The important thing is that we respect and support those who approach things differently, "so that the saints together make a unity in the work of service, building up the body of Christ."

By *contemplation* we mean the deliberate seeking of God through a willingness to detach from the passing self, the tyranny of emotions, the addiction to self-image, and the false promises of this world. It is a journey into faith and nothingness. The ordinary rules of thinking, managing, explaining, and fixing up the self do not apply here. It is a search for God, a love of larger Truth, and not the mere manipulation of ideas and feelings inside the private self. Contemplation is the "divine therapy" and the perennial clearing house for the soul. All the great world religions recognize its necessity in their more mature stages. For Christians, it is Jesus' sojourn in the desert for forty days and Mary's "Let it be done unto me according to your word" (Luke 1:38).

We all need vacations, leisure time, quiet time, and reading. But these are not necessarily the contemplative journey, and sometimes they actually keep us from it by excessive self-analysis, the need to work it all out, or the desire to avoid people and problems. Introverts have no natural head start into contemplation. Their busyness and control needs just take a different shape from those of the extrovert.

It is important that we continue to clarify and hold to these two pivots of our lives. Rightly sought, action and contemplation will always regulate, balance, and convert each other. Separately, they are dead-ended and trapped in personality. The clear goal of our Center is to meet people "where they are at" and help them trust "where they are not at." For all of us it is an endless rhythmic dance. The step changes now and then, but Someone Else always leads.

Powerful Impact

PAT SIMMONS

*M*y 52-year-old friend Helen has been diagnosed with Lou Gehrig's disease. What that means is that she could be dead soon.

A lot of people are drawn to Helen because she's a holy woman. Some recently expressed gratitude for her in a woman's circle. A Native American sister blessed Helen and the rest of us. We used dirt from a shrine at which miraculous cures are said to take place; we were smudged and we burned incense and candles. People shared from a depth we seem to reserve for times when we know the thread connecting life and the other world is fragile. Twenty women gathered; professionals—therapists, writers, organizers, program directors, social workers—a feminine powerhouse. Wonderful things were said and read and prayed. And Helen spoke.

Always, but more so since her diagnosis, Helen's words seem both sage and sacred. One woman mused afterwards that we should tape everything she says. But the most powerful words she spoke that day were in a simple question: "What if we die and God says, 'What I wanted you to do was play more'?" She then mused that she wasn't sure her thirty-plus years in the civil rights movement and human services work have made any difference at all. "That isn't what life is about. It's about friendship."

I tucked away the question and the statement to pull out when the Spirit moves me, because shamans gives us paradox and riddles to tease our souls onto the path.

The next week I ran into a friend who in partnership with another friend runs a program for troubled children and families. They work sixty or seventy hours a week, and the program has won many awards. It and they are outstanding. She shared with me that although she had just taken off three weeks from work, she was still tired. And although her partner and our friend was taking off two, she was aware of how fatigued she had become before she relented. So I said, "What if we die and God says, 'What I wanted you to do was play more'?" My lovely friend grew quiet and said with some resignation, "I can't turn away from all the suffering. There's so much suffering."

After that meeting, I reflected on Helen's words and recalled where I was two years ago. I was frenetically about the business of "saving the world." The summer of 1990 was a nightmare. A crisis at work led to two people sharing a work load originally planned for three. We were working on a summer conference for several hundred people. We had just opened a guesthouse to accommodate visitors. After the conference my staff partner in carrying this load left on a badly needed vacation. In a mindset somewhere between martyr and warrior, I gritted my teeth and tried to keep everything functioning while dealing with the stress of all the changes. In the antipode of thought-full living, I raced and ran, cajoled and persuaded, wrote and answered endless questions, dealt with guests and dropped when I got home after twelve-hour days. This was not the first time I had fallen into this pattern. I kept a similar schedule for years as a child advocate for abused and neglected children. It got worse.

When the other staff returned, I left with a daughter to drive five hundred miles one way to visit another daughter for a long weekend. It was much later before I could see the irrationality of that. Did I *need* a one-thousand-mile drive? Despite the questionable choice of diversion. I was glad to be free of the constant turmoil and overwhelming workload. By day four, I thought I had begun to deescalate my fifth gear attitude, but by then it was time to go home. I dropped my daughter off 180 miles east of Albuquerque, happy to spend a few hours of silence in the car.

I know now that I was neither relaxed nor slowed down. The truth was that I was misnaming emptiness and exhaustion.

Twenty miles later, living out a startling metaphor, I ran a stop sign and was struck by a GM truck. I remember thinking how surprised I was to be dying as I was hurled into a bridge, bounced off a pole and finally came to rest where I started but in the opposite direction. The car was totaled—damaged on all four sides. The left side of the motor had been violently relocated a couple of feet towards the passenger's side. Strapped securely in my seat, my demise would have been guaranteed if the truck had hit me a nanosecond later. Miraculously, nothing was broken or permanently damaged, but the force with which I was hurled left dark bruises along the outline of the safety belt. The truck driver was unhurt and the truck only slightly damaged. When I was released after an ambulance ride and X-rays, I asked my daughter to take me to photograph the car. I tend to have a short memory and even in my shock sensed the significance of this "accident."

I was talking to another friend last night. A dedicated physician—one who works too hard. So I asked her, "What if we die and find out that God wanted us to play more?" She sighed, and I shared the story of my automobile accident. With an Irish pun I remarked, "The accident had a powerful impact."

Later I reflected again on Helen's question in light of my very real admiration for the wonderful hardworking women I know. It seems to me that most human-services work and ministries are "on the backs" of women in midlife who are disproportionately "women who do too much." My brother who runs a five-hundred-bed mental health facility tells me that he'd have to close down without women in this age group. Do we acknowledge that we carry a terrible responsibility? And there is so much suffering!

But I don't work twelve-hour days anymore and I pay the price of guilt sometimes: I think about one in three Somalians dying because of famine and about death camps in Yugoslavia. I've companioned a young woman from an alcoholic family for five years as she grew from an at-risk preteen to a senior in high school. She's doing well now. Shouldn't I take on another needy child? Early on, the CAC started a once-a-month breakfast at a homeless shelter and a twice-a-month prison ministry. I no longer do either. I have a dear old friend in her eighties that I don't visit often enough. I heard a few months ago that the high-power lines in my neighborhood may be dangerous and the dirt in a vacant lot is toxic. I've been an organizer and a lobbyist. Couldn't I help? I don't attend all the demonstrations I'm invited to, and I respond only selectively to all the letters and petitions. I do care about environmental degradation, child abuse, sexism, racism, ageism, and all the other ways human beings have found to hurt one another. In fact, I sometimes ache over it all? But I know more truth than I can live, and, as Thomas Berry says in *Dream of the Earth*, "The ideal state for any individual or any culture is not exactly 'bovine placidity.' It is rather, 'the highest state of tension that the organism can bear *creatively*'" (my emphasis).

So I now officially work about forty hours a week on the CAC's agenda with a "preferential option" for social action and political reform. Priority setting by the CAC board of directors and staff gives me the gift of focus and a sense of hopefulness when we reach our goals. Maintaining friendships with workmates, friends, children, grandchildren, extended family, and the folks who come around the Center takes time, but Webster defines friendship as the state of being "fond of, intimate with, on the same side in a struggle, being supportive or sympathetic, helpful, reliable"— hardly the "leftovers" I used to save for when the important stuff was done!

I still take Dorothy Day's counsel, that if we are not victims of injustice, we must read or write about it so we don't deny it. I also believe as Ram Dass does that even if we cannot change evil, we must be willing to have our hearts broken again and again as part of our humanness.

I know that I've accomplished some important things in my thirteen years of child advocacy and five years with the CAC. But I live with paradox: No matter how indispensable or competent I might feel, I am only one of five billion persons on a planet which is one of one-hundred billion suns in our galaxy which is one of ten billion galaxies! Balancing this reality in creative tension with all I care passionately about and the things I can healthily accomplish feels closer to mind-full living for me. (I give myself enough grief without thinking I know what others should do!)

There are still days when I start to "gasp and pant" again, when I can feel myself "on a roll" getting sarcastic, judgmental, short-tempered, righteous, self-important, or downright unfriendly. Those are now red flags signalling the time to recall and remember my Self and the "powerful impact." What if I had died that day and God said, "Pat, I wanted you to play more ... and to be a better friend"?

On Being an Elder

DYCKMAN VERMILYE

I'm not sure how I should identify myself to others—or to myself. I'm just over seventy years old, and "middle age" just won't do. Henry Fonda, in *On Golden Pond,* made that crystal clear for me. When Kathryn Hepburn suggested that they might get together with some other "middle-aged friends," he exploded, "We're not middle-aged! People don't live to 150!" That clears the air on middle-age for me, but it raises the question about when that term is appropriate. Taken both literally and biblically, it suggests that the "M" word may be an affectation even for those who reach fifty. I suspect that we will see individuals over fifty as middle-aged and, in many instances, with good reason. We really are talking about an attitude toward life and growth related to *kairos* time as much as we are talking about *chronos* time and the yardsticks we use to measure distance from one point to another.

I envy women I know who have reached fifty. An increasing number of them are proud to reclaim the name and role of "crone." A book with that title had a wonderful subhead, *Women of Age, Wisdom and Power.* I think that is a good description of where many of us (men and women) want to be when we pass the half-century birthday. Some things happen that make wisdom and power accessible where it had not seemed within reach before.

But "crone" has been preempted. I found myself at a men's gathering several years ago, confessing in a large, closing circle that I was aware that something had changed in me—my perception of myself had changed. I was aware that my relationships with the men at that particular gathering—and my relationships with men elsewhere in life outside that setting—had taken a gentler turn from my earlier years. I was aware of less concern, less tension in relating. I was not as fearful of rejection or aggressive competition. I found it easier to talk about more than sports and children. I sensed a shift in my focus toward things that might be called spiritual. That clearly was a change in me. It puzzled me, and yet it was easy to observe and realize that it was right. I felt a need to ritualize that sense of movement in my life.

I shared these feelings and observations with those at the gathering, deplored the absence of a ritual that would allow a public recognition of the transition from one place on my life's path to another, and declared that I was therefore creating my own ritual right there and then—proclaiming myself to be an elder among them, and claiming a right to move up closer to the fire.

My declaration was coupled with an acknowledgment that I was now more ready than before to consider the responsibilities I had toward other, younger men. To be an elder was clearly not just all privileges of age: being given seats on buses, being "sirred," being moved to the head of the food line. It seemed to require as much activity as before, but in a different direction.

Since that evening ritual, I have been pleased to be part of other men's groups in which an explicit "crossing-the-fifty line" had been built into the planned program. Not acknowledged adequately for me is the apparent fact that this transition has been a part of other religions and cultures for a long time. The Hindu perception of a man's journey through life clearly marks out four successive periods: student, householder, hermit, and renunciant. The Native American cultures use elders for consultation, guidance, and wisdom when important matters affecting clan or tribe must be resolved. An apparent uncritical honoring of elders seems present in the Republic of China, where an uncritical respect for elders leaves the political leadership of the country in the hands of aged men. So "honoring" elders is not an automatic step. Considering how elders might be brought into the lives and resolution of problems of younger members of the society does seem right to me. It requires thoughtful consideration both by the man who wants to claim that place for himself and by younger men willing to create a cadre of men, older than themselves, to whom they might turn for advice, guidance, and friendship.

I find it wonderful to be part of the older contingent. I feel it a time for as much involvement, thinking, and growth as were earlier stages in my development. I feel in tune with the title of Mark Gerzon's recent book, *Coming into Our Own*. There are things I find I can do that I could not do easily before: be more honest; be more direct; get in touch with my feelings and share them; know where I am vulnerable and not be afraid to acknowledge that; tell my story without hesitation or embarrassment. It is a time for me of remarkable liberation. I hope it continues.

Monday Mornings at the Center

AVIS CROWE

*T*he week begins gently at the Center for Action and Contemplation, unlike so many other workplaces where Monday mornings can be harsh, as if one were emerging from a darkened room into the bright sunshine. There's frequently a rush to catch up with the mail and with tasks left incomplete on Friday. I can recall dragging wearily into many an office, already looking forward to the first coffee break and wondering what I was doing there in the first place! How different it is at the Center!

It's almost 7:30 a.m. on Monday. Inside the long, single-story building that houses the CAC, it is quiet, hushed, almost. I walk down the long carpeted corridor toward the collection of shoes outside the door of the prayer room, slip out of my sandals, adding them to the neat lineup, and step into the heartspace of the Center.

The room embraces me with its calm. It is a simple room, painted off-white with beige carpeting cushioned to welcome bare feet. The furnishings are sparse: a circle of wooden Zen prayer benches in the middle of the room and large, plump cushions around the wall. Overhead a vigil light flickers, casting soft shadows. A covered Native American pot containing the Eucharist sits in the center of the floor on a round rush mat. A rough-hewn crucifix brings the Hispanic world into our midst. It is a place of rest. Even when I go in during the course of a busy day, I find myself slowing down, emptying out, becoming more open, spacious, available. Hundreds have spent time there—each on a journey, each leaving behind their unique presence, their prayers, their yearnings for peace and justice and understanding of what it means to live in and by faith. It is a place of seeking, of letting go, of pilgrimage; it is sacred space.

I scan the dimly lit room to see who's there. Staff, interns, and visitors are seated cross-legged on the floor; several lean up against the wall; one sits on a small stool in the corner; others kneel, resting back on the little upholstered benches. I locate a vacant one, take a few deep breaths, and settle into the corporate silence.

At precisely 7:30, Christina strikes a small Tibetan temple bowl, its resonant vibrations calling hearts and minds together and into the presence of God. The Divine is always present, of course, in each of us and in the midst of us. Yet the sound of a bell or chime brings us to a keener attention.

For the next twenty minutes, we share the silence interrupted only by an infrequent late arrival and the soft sounds of breathing—like the soughing of the wind. In a trice or after an eternity, depending on where we are that particular day, the singing of the bronze bowl signals an end to this contemplative time together. We remain seated, stretch a bit, readjust our position, and greet one another quietly. I look around, wondering who will read the shared prayer this week. This responsibility rotates among us and the nature of the offering is very much a reflection of the intern or staff member who is leading. It usually begins with a reading of some kind—a passage of scripture, a poem, a story. The reader then offers some personal reflections, often followed by silence out of which anyone who wishes is invited to respond. One week it was the story of Zaccheus with some provocative questions that led to a rich personal sharing. A recent intern who was an enthusiastic bicyclist read an essay that used cycling as a metaphor for the journey of faith. We generally close this time with prayers and concerns that are in our hearts.

Now we begin to disperse. Interns and visitors leave, reclaim their shoes, and move off into Monday's tasks. Yet the staff is still not ready to shift into office routine. We remain in the chapel, the seven of us moving into a corner so we can be closer together, and enter into the third phase of the week's beginning, staff check-in. Each of us speaks about the background of our lives, what we are carrying with us as we go about our work that may be affecting our mood, our coping level, our stress quotient. It is a time of deep listening; a time to learn about one another, not only as coworkers but also as individuals with histories, families, dreams, even fear of things that go bump in the night. We discover that we can celebrate with one another, grieve with one another, laugh together.

There is no magic in any of this; we are by no means an ideal group of people, all working in love and harmony all the time. But it is a wonderful way to begin our week together, and it does help to create a kind of bond and empathy that keeps us at least a little more faithful to who we say we are. I can't help but wonder what might happen if every workplace would begin their week in a similar way. Not using our model, necessarily, but finding their own way to meet in small groups to share stories, concerns, the life-context in which they work. I suspect there might be some significant shifts in what takes place, both in the worker and in the workplace. I wonder.

Christ Against or Christ the Transformer of Culture

RICHARD ROHR, OFM

This article arose out of a discussion in which we pondered what the Christian response should be toward the 1988 presidential election. To what degree should we involve ourselves in partisan politics? At what point does separation from worldly political institutions become a witness to another reality of the Kingdom or merely separatist self-deception? As usual, the Gospel vision turns out to be more inclusive than our questions might suppose.

As we continue to reflect and educate in the area of social ministry, we also continue to confront a tension and a seeming conflict. How much do we resist, stand against, noncooperate, and offer a clear alternative to the systems of this World? And on the other hand, how much do we challenge, dialogue, negotiate from a position, and work with the system to effect small conversions from within? There are many implications once we make this choice. As always, there are strengths and weaknesses to both positions. What did Jesus do? What does the Gospel teach? We will seek some clarity on those questions in this short article.

Historically, of course, the general Western experience of Christianity has held neither of these positions! More often than not, we haven't stood against culture except in some areas of private morality, nor have we often critically challenged the culture except in those same areas of private morality or when the privileges or security of the church's self-interest were threatened. In general, we have equated the church's self-interest with the coming of the Kingdom.

We are finding it difficult to move beyond those patterns even today. Our people are accustomed to civil religion, cultural Christianity, where flag and cross seem to hang on the same pole. It never occurred to many Western Christians that religion should be anything else but the protector of law, order, king (or president!), crown, motherhood, and apple pie. When you don't follow that script, you look like a troublemaker, heretic, revolutionary—and all those other bad things that churchgoing people are not supposed to be. Our real position has usually been Christ *beneath* culture or Christ *at the mercy* of culture.

When empire doesn't have its way with Christ (that could be Roman, Holy Roman, Byzantine, French, Spanish, British, American, or Russian empires) beyond a few diversionary rituals and incense, there is simply no room for Christ. All we need to do is read the martyrologies of the first three centuries, the lives of Jesus, John the Baptist, Peter and Paul, Thomas à Becket, Thomas More, countless not so well-known saints (I wonder why?); plus the more recent totalitarian revolutions on both Right and Left. If the Sermon on the Mount gets in the way of the building and promoting of empire, you can guess which one goes. It isn't empire!

We really can't expect anything more of kings and queens, senates and presidents. Self-interested empire is what they are about. It is their business, although it does make me wonder how one can be really honest about their oaths of office and the Sermon on the Mount at the same time! The Sermon on the Mount supports nobody's empire and maintains nobody's self-interest. It points radically to another empire, which it says is absolute, and which Jesus freely calls *the* Kingdom.

But we can expect more of popes, bishops, clerics, and Christians. It is their surrender of the Gospel to the whimsy and demand of culture that I cannot comprehend or condone. Just today, I heard of a good bishop from the holy empire of California who told his seminarians that the present leader of the United States* was a good president and should be supported because he was good for the economy and "built up our defense." You wonder who the real heretics are, don't you? How is one supposed to respect such a man as an anointed teacher of the faith? He is apparently a materialist and has not reflected much on the mystery of the cross. Yet he is a bishop in good standing. Apart from any position on the merits and demerits of the presidency of Ronald Reagan, his criteria for judgment on that presidency are from the system and not from the Gospel. But it is not so hard to understand if your habitual approach to reading the Gospel is, "How can I fit Jesus into this given set of circumstances called American culture?" Again we have Christ at the mercy of culture.

Some Christian groups have tried to do it differently. First it was the monks, hermits, and anchorites—moving out of, away from, and against the demands of empire—and "anchoring" themselves to something and Someone more substantial. Then it became the various religious orders and movements, some within the Mother church, some without. But the common theme was a recognition that first you had to withdraw before you could engage effectively. You had to detach in order to attach, you had to deny before you could accept, you must empty out before Incarnation is possible. In very concrete and specific ways such as dress, economics, authority, ownership, sexuality, draft exemption, simplicity of life, mobility, accountability, and so on, Christian groups pulled apart from the dominant consciousness to exemplify a new way of living.

In Catholic circles, these lifestyles tended to take celibate form and lumped these values together in the name of "poverty, chastity, and obedience." In Protestant settings, Christians tended to move into radical lifestyle groupings like the Waldensians, Hutterites, Quakers, Shakers, Mennonites, and Amish. This was attractive to Catholic reformers like St. Dominic who told his friars, "Believe like the Catholics, but live like the Protestants." But in both of these cases, we see the consistent Christian recognition that there

---

ED. NOTE: Ronald Reagan

must be some kind of free choosing against the flow of culture. Now our questions are, "How much?" and "To what end?"

I have found considerable help in the two consistent literary styles that we find in the Scriptures: prophetic and apocalyptic. They are parallel and complementary attitudes. Although both have often been ignored or avoided by cultural Christianity, they are necessary for a full and dynamic reading of the word of God. Basically, the prophetic genre is a critical engagement of culture for the sake of its transformation. The prophets are usually enough a part of the church and political system to want to change it. Their message is reform, conversion, repentance. The apocalyptic genre says it's no use. The system is so corrupt, evil, and useless that you had best take your stand clearly and apart. Their message is revolution, disengagement, noncooperation, flee to God, faith, and the Absolute.

From these short descriptions you can see why both are dangerous and demanding attitudes. I don't think you can risk one without the other. They balance each other. Unfortunately, our usual stance was to avoid both! It demanded too much maturity and too much balancing. We settled instead for occasionally rigorous stands, usually in the area of body-life—sex, divorce, birth control, abortion, and celibacy—or, if you were Protestant, drinking, smoking, dancing, adultery, and pornography. It made us look prophetic, or even apocalyptic, without really risking very much or radically converting our attitude toward humanity, enemies, violence, success, or righteousness. We settled for being rigorous about a few things (feels good somehow) instead of being radical about the Reign of God.

The result has been disastrous for Western civilization: Power, prestige, and possessions move disguised and unquestioned among Christians. It is certain to happen when either the prophetic or the apocalyptic voice is ignored. Let's listen to these voices to hear what they have to say to us today.

The Prophetic Style

Although this word is used in many ways today, scripturally it is the language and stance of those Jewish figures who were very Jewish and very in love with and loyal to the best of their tradition. They were, in fact, so traditional that they were radical, so committed that they were critical, so at the Center that they appeared to be outside. But have no doubt about it: Elijah, Jeremiah, Amos, Micah, Nathan, Samuel, and Isaiah (and all the rest) were men of Israel, critically involved in its role in history, purifying its position and lifestyle so that it could speak the truth to the nations. Beginning with the prophetic charism of Moses, they were socially involved because God was apparently "socially involved"! Yahweh involved the power of God in their political issues of slavery and oppression. God took sides against the Egyptians and for their history.

The best of Judaism and its child Christianity has never allowed God to relinquish that position. An engaged and totally caring God called forth a socially engaged people. The prophets demanded such honesty of the people—and were never forgiven and always killed for it. Jesus the prophet saw the pattern very clearly and knew what would happen to him for trying to reform self-interested religion: "You are the descendants of those who murder the prophets! Very well then, finish off the work that your ancestors began" (Matt. 23:31–32). Yet the prophet never seems to give up on the people of God. For all of its hypocrisy and missing the point, the prophet knows that the gathered people of God is always and forever God's vehicle and instrument of salvation—and not righteous loners. The prophet is socially engaged, socially taught, and socially committed. Yahweh is not saving souls so much as Yahweh is saving truth in human history. The prophets, therefore, are not so much protecting individual rights and feelings as proclaiming God's rights on this earth.

As Abraham Heschel never tired of saying, the prophets are the passion and pathos of God in space and time. They are not the thought of God but the feeling, the pain, the ecstasy of God brooding over what is not yet full creation. The prophets try, work at it, suffer it, seek to cooperate with God in the transformation of the human situation, but from a position of radical criticism.

The Apocalyptic Style
It is important that we use this different word to distinguish carefully a language that is often confused with the prophetic but is very different from it. The apocalypticists are not the same as the prophets, although they do overlap, as in the books of Daniel and Ezekiel. We also see the apocalyptic style, along with the prophetic, in the words and manner of both John the Baptist and Jesus

himself, which is why we must take it very seriously. Finally, it is the chosen style of the book of Revelation, sometimes attributed to St. John the Evangelist. This book has caused much havoc in Christian history precisely because we have failed to distinguished it from prophecy and have thereby weakened its much more absolute position.

Basically, the apocalyptic style emerges to free God's people from taking themselves or their role in history too seriously. It says that after all is said and done (the prophetic function), give history back to God and be at peace in the transcendent truth. Don't try so hard that you become part of the bitter problem. The prophet might appear to be saying, "Work as if it all depends on you," the apocalyptic figure says, "Pray and trust as if it all depends on God." At the end of the day, cool it, forget it, and give history back to the Holy One who is going to achieve the victory anyway. The apocalyptic prophet has two simultaneous and self-correcting messages: (1) Everything matters immensely, and (2) it doesn't really matter at all. How many people do you know who can live out their lives on that pure and "narrow path"? I don't know very many at all. It seems that some are called to take the strongly apocalyptic position and all of the accompanying criticism in order to free the rest of us from our overengagement with and idolatry of "the way things are." Probably the most visible and effective witnesses to this position in our time are Dorothy Day and her "holy anarchy" and Thomas Merton's leaving it all to sit in a hermitage in the hills of Kentucky. They will always be open to criticism for not *doing* more, but their absolute stance, we have clearly seen, becomes the home and school for the emergence of true prophets.

Without the apocalyptic "No," prophets are no more than high-energy and idealistic activists, often working out of their own denied anger or denied self-interest. Apocalypticists are willing to be seen as fanatics, anti-American, anti-anything so that the rest of us can again discover the Absolute. They are bothered and bored by our relativities and rationalizations. They demand an objective Ground from which all else is judged and will not be nudged from their uncompromising stance. I believe one has to be a true and lasting contemplative to maintain the apocalyptic firmness and freedom.

Conclusion

Both the prophetic and the apocalyptic styles are necessary for the purification of the Judaeo-Christian tradition. The Gospel needs their capacity for self-criticism, and they need one another so that the Gospel can be both totally engaged and totally detached at the same time. The prophets are effective and relevant because of the freedom that absolute transcendence offers them. The apocalypticists are justified because they provide the clarity that healthy activism demands.

Predictably, we are assaulted today by both a false prophetic and a false apocalyptic position, which are always false if they are not balanced by the other sabbath rest. We see the pseudo-apocalyptic in the fundamentalist and charismatic types who love to use the "God will do it" and "God is great" language to cover their own intellectual and personal laziness. These are the heresies of the turned-on types in American Christianity today. They both have part of the necessary reform of Western Christianity. To the liberal and well-educated activist, the apocalypticist says, "Let go and let God. Surrender to mystery and Love." To the cozy charismatic, the prophet says, "Why would God give you something that you are not willing to work for yourself? Be honest, your vision of God's salvation is very small and very private."

To answer the question, "Should we get involved in the presidential election?" the biblical answer is "Yes!" (prophetic) and "No!" (apocalyptic). To the question "Should we work for the reform of the system?" the answer is also yes and no. Should we be hermits and refuseniks? Yes and no. Can we liberate the oppressed? Yes and no. Is life to be enjoyed and celebrated? Yes and no. Is life a sharing in Christ's cross? Yes and no.

Perhaps we should end as T.S. Eliot ended his classic poem, "Ash Wednesday":

> Suffer us not to mock ourselves with falsehood—
> Teach us to care and not to care . . .
> Our Peace in His will
> And even among these rocks.

Among these rocks of the human dilemma, our biblical answer is both an overriding No and an overwhelming Yes! We wait for such apocalyptic prophets.

THE BALANCING BIBLICAL VOICES

Apocalyptic Style	Prophetic Style
(Daniel, Ezekiel, John the Baptist, Jesus, Book of Revelation)	(Moses, all of the speaking and writing prophets, John the Baptist, Jesus)
It's God's world	It's our world
Christ against culture	Christ the transformer of culture
It's over	It's coming
Consolation	Confrontation
Powerlessness	Power
Absolutizes the Divine	Relativizes the human
Transcendent redemption	Immanent incarnation
Proclaims another reality	Works at this reality
Eternal	Temporal
God is victorious	God is suffering
Nothing really matters	Everything is important
Rest	Work
Separation	Solidarity
About the end of it all	About endings of each little part
Contemplation	Action

An Average Daily Life

PAT SIMMONS

> The here and now is all we have, any of us, out of which to make life worthwhile and God present and holiness a normal, rather than an unnatural, way of life . . . Spirituality is made out of the raw material of the average daily life. It assumes no great asceticisms and promises no great spiritual feasts . . . simply takes the dust and clay of every day and turns it into beauty.

I woke up a few weeks ago feeling out of sorts and looked up these words from Joan Chittister's book, *Wisdom Distilled from the Daily* (p. 6). The CAC staff has been reading and discussing this book, and this particular passage had been nagging at me.

Some time ago, I felt sure I had discovered my path to spirituality and holiness. (Just a tinge of arrogance there!) I had decided I would apportion a goodly amount of time each week to writing and exploring the great questions. Writing excites me, and sometimes ideas come to me with such rapidity that I'm sure that God's voice is in all this. I'd also been experiencing small awakenings about what a feminine spirituality might look like for me and was anxious to do more discernment. Everything feminine interests me because my goal is to learn to pull in, to be more vulnerable, soft, and reflective, and, even in the highest sense of the word, more passive. My temperament and experiences have led to a woman warrior life stance that has probably gone beyond the survival needs underlying that attitude.

I'm experiencing a growing passion for environmental concerns and am filled with ideas about how this can be integrated with spirituality. The concept of the world and all life as one living, breathing organism makes sense to me. And I also have a somewhat private agenda to become a contemplative in the vein of a Thomas Keating or Ruben Habito. (No half-measures here!)

So last April 12 was an important day. I moved into a townhouse in downtown Albuquerque to live alone for the first time in my life. I'd finally have time and focus to devote to my love affair with books and ideas. I was filled up with this fantasy of fruit-filled solitude; writing, reading, and interacting with others to trade philosophical concepts, wondrous witticisms, and anecdotes on our spiritual journeys. I'm fifty-three years old and it's time for me, I had decided, to pull back and be a sort of writer/wounded healer/crone/matriarch surrounded by books, candles, incense, and classical music. But this morning I am reminded of advice I gave a friend a few years ago: "You're spending your time yearning for a fantasy, missing the reality."

Exit Fantasy, Stage Right. Enter Reality.

Here's what I did last week: Sweated blood through my daughter's two days of labor, soothed a one-year-old grandchild separated from her mother for the first time, bit my lip repeatedly to keep from offering grandmotherly and probably romanticized parenting advice to my daughter, changed diapers, ran errands to the store, washed dishes, cooked, dealt with a leak in my new roof, supported a friend who's going through a crisis, talked to my other daughters who were physically walking through this journey with their sister, wrote my father who's been ill, worried about a son with the flu, answered some mail for some people who need support, and missed a contemplative seminar and a vigil to protest a New Mexico nuclear waste dump site. The latter two activities were the really important stuff happening that week. Or so I thought!

So what's going on here? I had determined that my life would be about reflecting on life's foibles, not living them! Where would the great spiritual mysteries of life be without my help? What about changing the environment and concerns about the dump site? Well, the only changes I was making were of the diaper variety, and the closest I came to a dump site was a diaper pail or cleaning up spilled food! What happened to the great Asceticisms and spiritual feats?

Joan's words nagged at me: ". . . spirituality is made of the raw material of the average daily life." There's another way to look at my week. I was aware and present to my own psychic pain and fears for my daughter in her difficult labor. I stayed with my grand-child, and met this child's late-night clinging to me with tenderness and compassion. I watched her trust in me grow, undoubtedly adding to the side of the scales that weighs towards her future ability to trust her world. I was there as my daughter put her new little girl child to her breast and saw her joy as she seemed to forget the forty-eight hours of hard work to bring her into the world. When my daughter got tense or irritable, I responded with charity instead of self-full defensiveness. My prayer that my disk-problem-prone back would serve me through all the lifting came from a deep place in my being. (I who on great and global levels strive to accept vulnerability!) I became increasingly aware that *this*—the raw, unprocessed, unrefined "stuff" of our daily life—is what spiri-tuality is about. Not the "stuff" that I'll do when I get my daily chores out of the way.

About the third day into this week, I was getting into my car at 6:45 a.m. to return to another day as mother's helper. I paused a moment, looked at the sky, and was suddenly aware that I was participating in sacred rituals that have gone on since time imme-morial: women gathering to care for those heavy with child and then remaining to soothe and hold and rock and treasure the new life. The particulars, yes, even the diapers and spills, are parts of a rite that is very primal, very human, very holy. Serving this pro-cess well and with presence and reverence is how I can be a wise mother. I have experienced four live births, a stillborn child, and a miscarriage and can be a wounded healer to my daughter's pain and fears. And any crone tendencies are in me because I've learned a lot about the cycles of life and death in my over fifty years. And someone even called me a matriarch recently, widowed ten years ago with four grown children, two sons-in-law, a daughter-in-law, and three granddaughters born in the last two and a half years! And I'll be darned, I am *writing* about all of this!

As Joan says, "The here and now is all we have, any of us, out of which to make life worthwhile and God present and holiness a normal, rather than unnatural, way of life. . . ."

Mending the Breach:
Inner and Outer Worlds

RICHARD ROHR, OFM

Only in the dual realm do voices become
eternal and mild.

                Rainer Maria Rilke, *Sonnets to Orpheus*

*I*n the early years of the New Jerusalem Community, the young
people loved to read and quote C. S. Lewis's *Chronicles of Narnia*.
They led me into wondrous adventures through magic wardrobes
into the land of Narnia. There the Christ-Lion Aslan reigned over
his kingdom and led the children of the story into battles and
brilliance and beauty. It was a journey through Christian parable
and mythology that has stirred my imagination to this day. When
Joseph Campbell came along and opened the meaning of myths to
so many Westerners, I could say, "I have been here before." Actually, I never left.

As the children leave the only world they ever knew, the door is
shut on Narnia as they fearfully answer the call to go "farther up
and farther in." Expecting to feel lost and alienated in a new land,
one of them instead says, "This is more like the real thing. . . .
Narnia is not dead. This is Narnia. . . . All of the old that mattered
has been drawn through the door into the real Narnia. . . . The
farther up and farther in you go, the bigger everything gets. You
see, the inside is larger than the outside." When we are no longer
totally distracted by the obvious (the outside) and perceive the
beyond and the depth of things (the inside), we are at last seeing
rightly and fully.

In C. S. Lewis's inimitable style, he is, of course, describing the
spiritual path. He is telling us not to be afraid to leave the familiar

and the customary for an inner world that is finally much more real and satisfying than the mere material world devoid of soul. How hard this is to believe when the outer world is a continuous display of color, sound, and intoxicating emotions! The outer Narnia, totally believed, becomes a prison. The inner Narnia fulfills and completes the outer.

Jesus seems clearly to prefer the inner vision as the prior and essential work, although this has often been used to avoid political and worldly involvement, which was not his intent. The inner movement is simply more radical, finally more comprehensive, and the easier to avoid. Ego has no problem disguising itself in outer good works; in the inner world ego stands revealed and worshipped. So Jesus says, "Alas for you . . . who clean the outside of the cup and dish and leave the inside full of extortion and iniquity. . . . Clean the inside of the cup and dish so that the outside may become clean as well" (Matt. 23:25–26).

The old temptation to operate out of "what the neighbors think" has taken on a contemporary form that is particularly seductive: political correctness. "PC" persons are still drawing their morality from outside themselves and anxious to look "right" among the appropriate people It seems to me that they are still living out of persona (mask) and not yet essence. To draw our identity around ourselves from outer voices is invariably to falter and fail in moments of crisis. In times of trial we need a rock-hard place to fall back upon. There is no such place for the mere politically correct. The result is whimsy, floundering, and indirection, unfortunately articulate every step of the way. Jesus describes his notorious cousin in opposite terms: John the Baptist is *not* "a reed shaking in the wind" (Matt. 11:7).

It is disappointing to me that I find this outer-directed personality as much among progressive and leftist types as among conservatives who have never internalized the law. At least conservatives have predictable and accountable reference points that they return to (even if one does not agree with them). The mere politically correct usually have no reference point except the recent wind which is restless, current, and often riding on guilt. It is also a house built on shifting sand. (Matt. 7:26).

Jesus describes the spiritual journey as a "narrow gate and hard path that leads to life," whereas the "road that leads to death is broad and wide" (Matt. 7:13–14). I do not think he is idealizing rigor or self-punishment; he is rather, distinguishing inner identity and inner authority (narrow gate and hard path) from that easy collective thinking that flows with the recent cultural mood. The way that everybody thinks today in my focus group is a "road broad and wide." It is the easy way to think, before praying, studying, or situating oneself in larger history. Remember, it was conventional wisdom that killed Jesus and all the prophets. Conventional wisdom held by the elites, who felt they were far above conventional wisdom!

As much as it is necessary and crucial for us to integrate the political question into our discussions and discernment, I see that it is also limiting if it is the only or even the prior question. If "Who has the power?" is your primary meaning question, I predict that you will not be a very pleasant person to be around. I often find that such people become negative, overly analytical, and carry an ever-ready chip on their shoulder—waiting, expecting, and seeing racism, sexism, oppression, and injustice everywhere. They are perhaps right, but they end up being dead wrong—within themselves and for a lot of folks around them.

It is very important that we ask the power-political questions, "Who is winner and loser here?", "Who has the power and should the power be realigned?", "Is it my job and call to realign that power right now?", "Am I supporting an unjust institution by cooperating here?", or even "Do I need to fight this power with an equal and opposing power?" But unless one is centered in God (I don't know what other word to use), such first questions usually pander to our control needs, our own sense of moral superiority, and an excuse to be aloof and noncompassionate—all of which is unseen and unaccountable because I am so "right." I have found this camouflage in myself and in far too many peace-and-justice types when we do not walk the path of personal transformation. Change agents who are not first of all committed to transformation are, frankly, a problem.

As we face our own inner Herods and Hitlers, we both recognize their disguises in others and we learn a certain forgiveness that is necessary for ongoing political involvement. I am *always* a part of the problem. I can never really stand apart, above, or beyond human sinfulness. I am a part of the tragic sense of life, and there is no perfect orthodoxy on which to stand.

We who are working for social change and justice must be willing to address our own idols and recognize the sometimes half-truths in the voices of our accusers. Maybe whole truths! Dare I list a few that I have heard? Some of them have been rightly directed at me:

1) Sometimes we seem to substitute an "ism" or ideology for religious faith, but treat it with the same unquestioning awe. Witness people's devotion to liberalism, the primacy of freedom, even when the common good is clearly suffering; witness women's addiction to the feminist analysis as if all ego and domination would be gone from the world if only women had control; witness the knee-jerk antiauthoritarianism of most Westerners; witness the worship of individualism as a substitute for the riskier tasks of individuation and community building. These are all forms of secular "faith" with many congregations of fervent believers.

2) Sometimes we seem to transfer our control needs from concern about content to preoccupation with and control of the process itself. We can then look very open and broad-minded, but in fact our dogmatism has just moved to how, when, and where, instead of what.

3) Sometimes we cannot be relied upon in terms of basic loyalty and perseverance through hard times. When personal growth and "wholeness" are the Gospel instead of the paschal mystery, it will be very hard to build anything enduring or stable. Yet the psychology of growth is only appropriate for the first half of life; in the second half of life the task is diminution and grounding. Many "growths" in the second half of life are cancerous. If that statement seems shocking, I am not referring to healthy growth forced by situations beyond our control: pain, humiliation, all the hurts of life that can lead to surrender and real honesty about limitations. Rather I mean "growth" directed by our ego and fashioned by our own definition.

4) Leftist or liberal thinking can lead to its own list of orthodoxies and heretics. It seems it is important to be tolerant toward all people and lifestyles except conservatives who are often disdained, certain Roman Catholics and fundamentalists considered naive or simple because they appear to be happy in their beliefs, and some men in authority who are presumed to be uncaring and insensitive. These groups are considered acceptable targets of jokes and criticism in many educated and liberal circles. Strange.

We are not off the hook of grace that easily. Grace holds us in the unenviable position of the prophet, "hung" in the dilemma of things, crucified on the conjunction of opposites. No wonder there are so few prophets!

Karl Barth, the German Protestant theologian, described the need for some anchor outside culture, outside history, outside personality, some North Star by which the private self can be guided:

> The Christian Church must be guided by the Word of God and by it alone. It must not forget for an instant that all political systems right and left alike, are the work of men. It must hold itself free to carry out its own mission and *to work out a possibly quite new form of obedience or resistance* (emphasis mine). It must not sell this birthright for any conservative or liberal mess of pottage.

The word of God might best be described as those inner and outer truths that are so urgent and authoritative that I cannot disobey them without calling it sin or even losing my soul. Persons without such a center and ground and calling power are condemned to those undisciplined squads of emotions and meanings that come from everywhere and go nowhere. We are capable of more than that.

The word of God relativizes and limits all worldly expectations and therefore liberates us for a bigger picture. It tells us that neither Bill Clinton, nor Ross Perot, nor George Bush will usher in the Reign of God. It tells us that neither the winners nor the losers have the whole truth, that there are no official explanations that will finally and fully "explain." Everything in this world is transitory, tentative, and not to be worshipped as God. When the outer/obvious is dethroned and relativized, we are capable of seeing the hidden wholeness of things, the inner Narnia that gives the outer its soul, its vitality, its full beauty. The word of God calls us farther up and farther in. It does not call us to be inner, "spiritual," or religious, so much as it calls us to be who we are, all that we are, and responsible for who we are. Which means we will allow others the same, and also work for their full humanity. This is the work of justice. It recognizes that we are not human beings who must become spiritual. We are already spiritual beings who are desperately trying to become human. The word of God holds us accountable to our own full humanity, which is God's unique creation.

This is also obedience. This is the true spirituality, but so integrated that it just looks like life—fully human—and therefore of God.

From such an inner world I can sally forth like Don Quixote, I can risk my wealth and reputation because I now possess it at much deeper levels, I can move into foreign and new territory because I radically belong, and this world is a good, if passing, home. I can work for tenant organizing, world hunger, and reforestation precisely because these outer tasks are an extension of my inner discovery. I don't need to succeed, I just need to act. I know ahead of time that I will not fully succeed, and my "rewards" are not all in the system.

Finally, the world and I are mirrors of each other, a universal I-Thou relationship. It names me and I name it. It creates me and I create it. It frees me and I free it. It loves me and I love it—till finally there is no significant inner and outer; there is "only Christ loving himself" (St. Augustine). If it still feels like two worlds, two journeys, two hungers, two loves, don't believe it! We must still go farther up and farther in. The most personal is finally the most universal.

If we are a "school for prophets," as some have called us, no shorter or less perilous journey is offered us. All that really matters will be drawn through the door.

Thanksgiving Reunion

AVIS CROWE

I've always identified with Mary in the Bible story of the two women hosting a gathering of friends to hear Jesus. Like Mary, I would have chosen to sit at the feet of the teacher, deaf to any call for help from the kitchen. She is presented as a woman of radiance and inner peace, in touch with what truly mattered and able to give herself totally to the present moment. She is the model contemplative, the very picture of the woman I long to be to the point of deluding myself into believing I am. (Unlike Mary, I would have had a notebook in hand, determined to "catch" the pearls as they fell so I could reflect on them further, perhaps write a piece for *Radical Grace!*) It seemed to me that Martha's constant activity and cranky clattering about kept her from giving full attention to the beloved Teacher. Why didn't she simply put down the dishes and join the others? Why so much fuss and bother? Poor misguided Martha, so busy doing, she was missing the best part. I couldn't understand her at all. Until last Thanksgiving.

My husband and I were looking forward to the holiday, having invited a group of friends to share it with us. I was to have minimal responsibility as my husband was to take charge of the turkey and trimmings and several guests were to bring side dishes. My contribution would be a favorite casserole that I could prepare ahead of time, general helping out, and playing hostess. Circumstances abruptly dictated a change of scenario that cast me grudgingly into another role and brought me face to face with an aspect of myself I don't much like.

My husband had returned from a weekend trip and announced on Monday morning that he wouldn't join me for our regular swim; he was tired and had decided on a quiet morning at home. I was later than usual getting back, and when I walked into the house, a wan voice from the bedroom announced trouble. The "quiet morning at home" had included some heavy yard work, bringing on a crippling attack of back pain. He had barely been able to drag himself to bed where I found him, flat out and in agony. I seesawed between compassion and annoyance. He had wrenched his back before and knew better than to do the kind of physical labor he'd taken on that morning. Inside I was seething. Thanksgiving was just three days away and six people were coming for dinner. The idea that I might have to do the whole thing appalled me. Hard to believe, but at fifty-plus, I'd never cooked a turkey in my life! Though I was unaware of it at the time, Martha had just asserted herself.

I suggested calling everyone and canceling; I was sure they would understand. But my bedridden spouse insisted he would be up and around in a day or so and able to handle the bird as planned. Against my deeper instincts, I agreed. But by Wednesday it was clear that not only would he not be able to do any cooking, he would probably not be able to get out of bed. We still could have called it off, but such a last-minute cancellation seemed mean-spirited. I voiced my continuing anxiety, but my husband the chef convinced me the turkey would be a "piece of cake," and I summoned up some positive thinking. I was determined not to be done in by a holiday dinner for eight.

I made a few calls to explain the situation and enlist some help: George to carve the bird; Karen to make gravy. Everyone was sympathetic, eager to come, and willing to pitch in. I enjoyed planning seating arrangements so my husband wouldn't be isolated. I set up a card table and three chairs in the bedroom so half the guests could be with him while the others would be with me in the dining area. We would switch places for dessert. To simplify things I would ask guests to serve themselves from the kitchen counter. I took part of the dried flower arrangement I'd prepared for the table and created a second small one, and found another candle and holder. I wanted the "make-do" table to be festive and attractive, too. I began to feel less nervous.

By the time people arrived, I was reasonably calm. There had only been one crisis as I was preparing the turkey. I simply could not get the wretched thing trussed up properly, the thin skin kept tearing, the legs refused to tuck in the flap, the slippery carcass kept sliding out of my grasp. I was grateful no one was around to watch as I did battle with the poor creature. Tears, held back for days, streamed down my face. My silence, curt replies to queries from the bedroom, and an occasional louder-than-necessary snuffle gave me away. My husband called me to him, held out his arms, inviting me to let it all out. While he held me I gave in to a good cleansing cry. The bird that went into the oven didn't look at all like the pictures in magazines, but my bout of weeping over, we had a good laugh and agreed that it would no doubt taste just fine!

Dinner arrangements were in place but I hadn't thought about pre-dinner socializing. I had guessed we'd all have a pleasant time visiting over drinks in the living room, guests popping into the bedroom one at a time to greet the invalid. However, when my "helpers" arrived, they left their food offerings on the counter, received drinks with thanks, and after proper "call me when you need me" noises, disappeared into the bedroom with a platter of veggies and dip. They perched on the bed and chairs, settling in for the duration. Too polite to shoo them away and at least partly enjoying the role of incapacitated but genial host, my husband held court while I felt abandoned in the kitchen and began to roast along with the turkey as I started to put dinner together with a heavy hand. Damn his back, anyway!

I set about my self-assigned tasks with determination, noisily preparing the serving area, dumping mini-marshmallows on the sweet potato casserole, checking on the turkey, and mentally ticking off what had yet to be done before we could eat. Images of my mother hovered over me. As the minister's wife she was a gracious hostess but inclined towards severe anxiety behind the scenes, especially when company was expected. Pots and pans would pile up in the sink. I would be dispatched to set the table and see that the appropriate serving dishes and utensils were at the ready while mother tried to orchestrate the various cooking times so everything would be done at the right moment. I don't recall much pleasure in the whole process and came to experience the kitchen as a place to avoid. I've overcome much of that resistance, but under stress it all comes back. I rushed about, nervously calculating when the turkey would come out of the oven and wondering when to call Karen to make the gravy so it would be ready at the same time. I might as well have been my mother forty years ago! I was anything but thankful, and with sounds of good-natured chatter and an occasional outburst of laughter drifting in from the nearby "sickroom," I felt more and more frustrated, angry, and put upon.

I suspect it would have been all right to put things in the kitchen on hold and join the party in the other room. No one would have minded if dinner was delayed, and it probably would have been fine to serve peanut butter sandwiches! Years ago, during time spent at a community in rural Georgia, I had learned that hospitality wasn't so much about what food you cooked, how much there was, or how elegantly it was served. It was about being with one another, about sharing stories of the journey, about breaking bread together. I seemed to have forgotten that lesson and was unable to let go of my own agenda and the distorted need I felt to make it all "work." I forged ahead, telling myself it would all be over in a few hours.

Finally I called on my helpers to join me in the main arena. (I thought they came rather reluctantly; by this time my attitude was thoroughly uncharitable.) George painstakingly dismembered the turkey; Karen created a fine gravy, confessing it was her first! It looked like we would sit down to a Thanksgiving feast after all. Everyone filled their plates and reorganized themselves at the two tables. The bird came out the way it was supposed to; the apple/cornbread/sausage stuffing elicited exclamations of pleasure; Robyn's cranberry whatever was superb. I relaxed into the pleasure of the moment, breathing a sigh of relief. I had done it!

The moment passed quickly. I began worrying about keeping the food hot for seconds, about whether my husband was managing to eat all right in his nearly prone position, or whether he was in pain. I wondered when I should put the pie out, I wondered, God help me, how long it would be before everyone would finally leave. Up and down, checking on this and that. I acted out a caricature of the perfect hostess while behind that facade I felt as if I were about to burst into a thousand fragments.

Without warning, that biblical scene flashed vividly into my head. Only this time I knew myself as Martha. Gone was the contemplative Mary, and in her place was the Martha the hyperactive. Martha! That compulsive doer who insisted everyone should do things her way! Surely that wasn't me! I couldn't bear it. Yet in that moment I knew her to be me as surely as I knew anything. It was as if I had suddenly become aware of a long ignored twin. By insisting on identifying with Mary and "taking the better part," I had been blind to Martha, unwilling to claim any aspect of that overly busy, anxious-to-please woman. Tired of being denied, she marched into my kitchen to say, "Hey! Pay attention to me!" With a little help from my beloved spouse, she had elbowed Mary out of the way completely, demanding her due. A difficult leap for me to make; I'm much more comfortable being Mary. But as I grudgingly began to make room for this neglected sister of mine, I could see a lifelong pattern of choosing one over the other—with Mary the clear favorite. This had been unintentional, even unconscious. Now that I had been forced to "see" with more than my eyes, I understood Mary and Martha to be sisters, inner twins. I still like Mary better but realize that I must learn to honor and nurture Martha too. Both have gifts to offer, and for them to live in harmony I must learn to receive them with grace and gratitude.

As I stood in the doorway watching the guests drive away, I felt some inner peace return. As Mary sighed with contentment and relished the fleeting moment of insight with humor and resignation, Martha was replaying the whole evening and getting ready to wash the dishes and straighten up the house. Did Mary have the better part? It was, after all, the neglected, uninvited sister who had barged in on Thanksgiving to teach me something of my own truth and challenge me to own a part of myself I had long rejected. Just how well we'll get along is still to be played out. But for a moment, anyway, I felt very benevolent and could say with conviction, Welcome home, Martha. Welcome home.

About the Authors

Sue Brown is an Albuquerque pediatrician and former CAC board member. She lived in Haiti for six years.

A former librarian, teacher of creative writing and 1991 CAC intern, **Justine Buisson** is semi-retired and lives in Miami, Florida. She is a published poet and devotes much time to volunteer work, Pax Christi, and the South Florida Peace Coalition.

Eileen Burke, co-editor of the CAC's newspaper, *Radical Grace,* is a graduate of the University of Maryland who worked as a reporter for several daily newspapers before marrying and raising a family. She now lives in Albuquerque.

Maria Reis Habito lives with her husband, Ruben, and two young sons in Dallas, Texas, where she teaches part time at Southern Methodist University. Originally from Germany, she met Ruben in Japan where they both studied with the same Zen master.

Linda Hardy has a degree in medicine and has worked as a newspaper photographer and reporter. She lives in Austin, Texas, with her husband and two sons. Her current passion is songwriting.

The former manager of the CAC's guest house, Tepeyac, **Marie Nord** is a Sister of St. Francis of Rochester, Minnesota. She is committed to living gently on the Earth and has been a vegetarian for over twenty years.

Gerald Ortiz y Pino is a native New Mexican, a social worker with 25 years' experience in that field, and a member of the CAC's board of directors. He has been involved with the Albuquerque Coalition for El Salvador for three years and has been a volunteer at St. Martin's Hospitality Center for seven years.

Michael Roche is a husband, father of three, professor, attorney, author, prison educator, and international service worker. For over twenty years he has taught at the University of South Dakota. He offers workshops and presentations to interested groups on nonviolence, compassion, education and professionalism. For several years Dr. Roche has spent summers traveling to a number of other countries, usually in a service capacity.

The founder and animator of the CAC, **Richard Rohr** is a Fanciscan priest, author of books and cassette tapes, and internationally known speaker. His retreats and programs around the world particularly focus on the integration of contemplation and justice and peace work, and he is greatly appreciated for his wise reflection on so many issues which currently challenge Church and society.

A CAC co-director for five years, **Pat Simmons** came to the Center after fifteen years in human services administration, including several years as director of Big Brothers/Big Sisters of Albuquerque. A widowed mother of four and grandmother of four, Pat currently lives in a rural area near San Antonio, Texas.

Kent Smith is an ordained Presbyterian minister who spent several years as a supervisor of clinical pastoral education and was executive director of Gould Farm, a residential psychiatric treatment program in Massachusetts, from 1972–1991. He worked on the CAC staff from April to December, 1993.

Jack Tischhauser and his wife currently live in San Diego, California, where they are involved in the Catholic Worker, Pax Christi, and Network. He is also very active in the Contemplative Outreach Organization founded by Abbot Thomas Keating.

Mary Vineyard is a mother, message therapist, and poet who lives in Albuquerque. She has been involved at the CAC since its beginning.

Avis Crowe Vermilye makes her home in Corrales, New Mexico, with her husband, Dyckman. A CAC staff member and member of the Religious Society of Friends (Quakers), Avis writes and leads retreats and workshops on aspects of the spiritual journey and contemplative living. Her work has appeared in *Radical Grace, Fellowship Magazine, Friends Journal,* and *Fellowship in Prayer.*

A former staff member of the CAC, **Dyck Vermilye** luxuriates in retirement as an official "cuddler" in the intensive care unit of the neonatal clinic at University Hospital in Albuquerque. He is also a court appointed special advocate for children whose parents are before the court on charges of child neglect or abuse.

A nutritionist, author of several books and macrobiotic counselor, **Rebecca Wood** lives in Albuquerque with her teenage daughter. She regularly presents workshops at the CAC and elsewhere on the healing and medicinal properties of food.

About the Editors

Teddy Carney lives and works on a cattle ranch in California with her husband. She is an occasional writer and volunteers in a group that helps with the needs of farm laborers and their families.

A CAC co-director since 1988, **Christina Spahn** spent six years as director of religious education for the Archdiocese of Santa Fe. She has authored four books of workshops on various aspects of spirituality and ministry and has been managing editor of *Radical Grace* for the last several years.